LI[illegible]

POCKET

OF

CONFIDENCE

TEN GOLDEN STEPS

RAJ SOREN

LITTLE POCKET OF CONFIDENCE

Published By:

Dream Publications

Dream Publications
Sarkheldih,
Jamtara,
Jharkhand. 815351
India.

www.DreamPublications.net
editor@dreampublications.net

ISBN: Paperback: 978-81-938898-4-8
ISBN: EBook: 978-81-938898-5-5

Cover Page Painting: Chandni Soren

First Publication 2020

RAJ SOREN

LITTLE POCKET OF CONFIDENCE

Ten Golden Steps

If you wish to contact the author:

Raj Soren,
Email-confidence@pdss.co.uk

Dedicated to Everyone in Need.

PREFACE

I have written this book "Little Pocket of Confidence – Ten Golden Steps" just for you after considerable thought and research. I have put together tried and tested methods to help you increase your confidence and self-esteem. The book is designed to help you in your journey to a greater self-confidence and a more fulfilling life. If you are already super confident then that's great maybe you can pick some useful tips to help and support others less confident than yourself.

This information will give you a step by step approach of how to look and feel more confident in many aspects of your life whether it is in a job interview, managing and leading people, speaking in public or making new friends or even being a better parent.

Confidence is such an important part of our lives that the lack of it can be crippling and it can have a devastating effect on how we perform at work or in business and our personal lives. Whether you are a manager or CEO of a company, a teacher, a doctor a solicitor, a mother, a father, a husband, a wife a teenager or a grandparent, low confidence and self-esteem can affect us no matter who we are.

Having the right level of confidence to tackle the daily challenges that life throws at you is vital in dealing with these issues with ease and self-assurance. Growing up as the only Indian boy or person of any color in school of 1200 students had its own challenges. I had good upbringing and family support and even though I private tutors I still struggled at school and was slow learner but an attentive and hard worker. I failed exams on a yearly basis and had to retake English 3 times in my school years at age 16 and 18 I had to retake exams. I failed biology and chemistry which had a big knock on my confidence. My brother and sister excelled at school and I was happy for them because I had my own path to walk. After retaking my exams, I just managed to do get on to an Applied Biology diploma at University and then later completed a degree in Biology and chemistry. I failed more job interviews then passed but later succeeded in sales, training and management career. Some 15 years later I passed my master's degree in business and social entrepreneurship while still working a full-time job. I feared speaking in public and would sweat profusely and my legs would feel like jelly with my vocal cords tightening so much that I couldn't speak up. I am now able to speak to hundreds of people at one time. In sports I was one of the worst in my Ju Jitsu class when I first started in 1984 and I couldn't remember the Japanese technology. I would get very dizzy when I was asked to do Ju Jitsu rolls in class because I suffered from dizziness yet I persisted and became national champion over a number of years and then a senior black belt teaching nationally and internationally as part of The Jiu Jitsu Foundation. I also gained a second black belt in Aikido in my mid-50s. My three children all now adults also have gained Ju Jitsu black belts which I am very proud of. I am privileged to run one of the most successful Ju Jitsu clubs in our organization with the support of my wife and co-instructors. I gained a LIFE coaching to diploma to help people improve their confidence and with their goal setting and supporting the work of the Mind charity.

Why do I share this background with you well it's because I had my own struggles and a big knock in my confidence and self-esteem and having to overcome bullying and racism in my early years? I had to learn to be a father a husband and sales manager in my career as well as a martial art instructor. I have experienced some of the same challenges and knock in confidence that you are going through so I can relate and better offer some help and advice.

Therefore, I have developed 10 steps to increase your level of confidence. These can be thought as the 10 GOLDEN STEPS for courage and a braver heart. I am confident that you will take and apply some of these steps to help improve your own confidence and better your personal circumstances and open the world to more opportunities.

I have taken each letter of the word confidence to represent an important chapter in this book.

Confidence comes from having

1. C -Courage
2. O -Overcome
3. N -Negativity
4. F -Feelings
5. I -Inspiration
6. D -Determination
7. E -Esteem
8. N -Necessity
9. C -Communication
10. E -Enthusiasm

I will be discussing these 10 Golden steps with you and as you read and study each chapter you will be picking up valuable golden nuggets of information and tips. I will be illustrating this journey of self-discovery with stories and sharing some personal experiences as well as tried and tested advice that have worked for me and for many others.

So, what makes one person more confident then another and what allows them to have more courage to achieve great many things in life, read on and discover the answers.

ACKNOWLEDGEMENT

I want to thank my wife Jyoti for always believing in me and for the idea of the book title. Also, to my children Suraj, Chandni and Lukhi for their encouragement. To my parent's Dr Dhuni Soren and Mrs. Bhagwati Soren for their love and support.

Thank you, my publishers, Amit and Esha Besra at Dream Publications.

www.DreamPublications.net

CONTENTS

Chapter 1

CONFIDENCE: C for **COURAGE**

"You gain strength, courage, and confidence by every experience in which you really stop to look fear in the face. You are able to say to yourself, "I have lived through this horror. I can take the next thing that comes along." . . . You must do the thing you think you cannot do." Eleanor Roosevelt

Lion and the hyena

First let me tell you a story which is set in continent of Africa about courage.

It was another hot day on the plains of the African savannah. The wilder beast grazed in their thousands interspersed with Zebra, antelope and gazelles. A line of elephants took their turn at the watering hole with the bull elephants taking large trunk full of water and spraying their backs to cool themselves from the scorching sun.

Close by there were two figures hidden under the shadow of a large tree overlooking this spectacle. One of them was a tall elderly tribesman who was a grandfather and his name is Jabari and he sat with his grandson Diallo. The grandfather was the chief of the local tribe and he was out with his grandson and mesmerizing him with his stories of the hunts that he used to go on when he was a younger man. Diallo listened tentatively so he could learn from his grandfather's wisdom.

So why am I telling you this story. I believe that we can all learn and remember far better from listening to stories, so you will find several stories featuring in this book.

Getting back to the story well the grandfather's name **Jabari** means **Fearless** or **valiant** and the grandson's **Diallo** means **brave one** which is very apt for these character.

Drawings by Jyoti Soren

Jabari and Diallo noticed a lion and a hyena were also roaming the plains. The grandfather spoke in a calm and soothing voice and told his grandson.

"The Lion is brave and courageous beast and the hyena is cunning"

"The hyena is also a strong beast that can cause problems for the lion and to man since hyenas are very strong when they hunt in large packs"

Diallo asked his grandfather "Who would win in a fight if the hyena was to fight the lion?"

The grandfather replied,

"The one that would win is the one who is the stronger in heart, body and mind."

Diallo replies, "Would that mean that the lion would always win "

Grandfather responds,

"A large fit lion would always win a fight against one hyena however this same lion would lose if for one brief second he doubted his own strength and abilities then he would be overcome be weakened by the cackling sounds of the hyena and its evil stare"

When Hyenas hunt in large packs and even a brave lion is no match for them.

"The grandfather said in our hearts we are all lions but when people laugh and mock us we become timid and scared and our brave and courageous hearts can be changed to that of a young deer and we are soon overcome by the hyenas of this world"

Hyenas can almost be thought of as people that laugh at what you do and what you are trying to achieve in life. The sound of laughing and cackling hyenas might even represent the negative people in your life who may say things like what do want to go to college, why do you want to move out of the city for, why do want to move jobs, why do want to change the way we work. Many people get into a comfort zone and don't like others changing the status quo.

I have shared this story to help illustrate a point about that human nature can sometimes be close to those of the animal kingdom. When we are seeking to be confident in our daily lives, we sometimes face internal fears that we allow to become barriers to achieving certain things in life like presenting in public, going for a promotion at work or dealing with seemingly difficult people. There are also several external factors that we must deal with in order to fulfill our goals in life like the way we react to other people and difficult circumstances such as losing a job or having problems in business.

These problems and fears that face us on a day to day basis are like the laughing hyenas. Imagine for a moment that these hyenas represent negative thoughts. Negative thoughts are like hyenas in that they hunt and attack in large packs in the recesses of your mind and they can soon overwhelm you causing you to lose your confidence and doubt yourself. In our hearts and minds we can have two beasts that represent our poor self-image or a confident and more reassuring one. The Lion can represent the positive strong and brave beast and the Hyena as the negative and evil that undermines our abilities and thoughts.

If we feed the Lion with positive thoughts and self-belief, then we too become stronger to face more challenges. The hyena becomes stronger if we allow it to dominate our lives thus allowing it to grow in negative thought and influence.

So how can you overcome and manage these negative thoughts and keep even these 'hyenas' at bay?

The story of the Lion King is one of Disney's more popular films illustrates this idea of Hyena versus Lion. The lion from the famous story of the Wizard of Oz was searching for courage however courage was always in its heart and it did not need to search for it.

One way to kill the hyenas is to starve them of negative thoughts and drown them with positivity self-belief and positive affirmative actions. No longer will the packs of hyenas roam your thoughts and they will die or seek other plains in weaker minds. I will cover positive affirmations later in this book and how to reframe negative thoughts.

In some people's minds negative thoughts may develop as a result of external factors that happen around them at work business or home life or something deep seated that has festered for some time as result of a traumatic experience. There may be someone close to you such as a work colleague or possibly a friend or members of your own family that are causing negative influence. It's most likely it's in their nature to do so and they have been acting this way for some time. You may have even wanted to do something different with your life and these people try to stop you achieving what you want. They are like anchors from holding you back from sailing the seas of adventure or even the chains holding you back from flying to dizzy heights of success. These could well be the same people that sap way at your energy.

How will you find your courage?

Confidence and courage come in many forms, take for instance the 1995 Oscar winning film Braveheart staring and directed by Mel Gibson. Mel Gibson plays a 13th century warrior who becomes famous for his speech at the Battle of Sterling and he gained recognition for waging the first war for Scottish independence against King Edward the I of England also known as Longshanks.

Wallace was truly brave to oppose the King and his motivation was driven as a result of the death of his wife Murron. Wallace is drawn into this battle as a result of English soldier who tries to attack his wife Murron. Wallace fights off several soldiers and the two of them attempt to flee but Murron is captured and sadly executed by the village sheriff. This sheriff now proclaims, "An assault on the King's soldiers is the same as an assault on the King himself." In retribution, Wallace and several villagers slaughter the English garrison and execute the sheriff. Wallace now finds himself compelled to rebel against the English.

Wallace's brave and motivation speech stirs his men into battle.

"I am William Wallace. And I see a whole army of my countrymen, here in defiance of tyranny!

You have come to fight as free men.

And free man you are! What will you do without freedom? Will you fight?"

"Two thousand against ten?" - the veteran shouted.

"No! We will run - and live!"

"Yes!" Wallace shouted back. "Fight and you may die. Run and you will live at least awhile.

And dying in your bed many years from now, would you be willing to trade all the days from this day to that for one chance, just one chance, to come back here as young men and tell our enemies that they may take our lives, but they will never take our freedom!"

This was his motivational speech to his men before battle which helped his men overcome fear and gave them courage that stirred their hearts and souls to battle to the death and eventually win. We all know how history has changed since those days. The good thing is that we do not have to take on any major battles like Wallace had to, yet we have our own battles to fight and our own courage to ignite. We can all be brave when we need to be, it depends on our level of conviction and the ability to overcome our own internal self-doubting dialogue and beliefs.

"Life is like swimming in the river, but it takes courage and immense effort to get to the other side. You must battle against the currents along the way, but you become stronger as a result."

In many situations its fear of the unknown that prevents us from acting.

What type of fear is possibly holding you back?

I would recommend a book call "Feel the fear and do it anyway" by Susan Jeffers

There are many types and forms of fears that present no life threat, these include.

- Fear of rejection

- Fear of being judged
- Fear of change
- Fear or spiders, heights animals
- Fear of darkness
- Fear of failure
- Fear of closed spaces
- Fear of heights
- Fear of public speaking
- Fear of speaking to others
- Fear of success
- Etc.

All these fears can be overcome if you believe and work on overcoming them.

You can gain more courage by regularly working on it, like a muscle the more you exercise the muscle the stronger you become.

People can sometimes think that courageous people have no fear this is not true it's just that they have had more practice at dealing with them over their lifetime. These individuals' still get nervous and anxious, it's their ability to keep moving forward even if they are afraid.

In the jungle we can sometimes step on a stick and jump in fright thinking it was a snake. The fear was not real however it initiated a real response.

Let me tell you about an incident a few year ago when I was cleaning an old shed. As I was cleaning, I felt something creeping up my leg. I moved my leg the thing that was creeping up my leg kept moving higher and faster up my leg. I didn't know if it was a large spider or small rat or even a snake. I became so worried that I ran out of the shed and pulled my trouser down to try and get rid of this animal or insect on my leg. What I discovered was that it was not a rat or spider after all but a tree twig that had got caught inside my trouser leg. My wife was in the garden at the time cutting the grass and all see saw was her husband running out of the shed with trying to take off his trouser which was a comedy moment which she relived for many years afterwards. In this situation my mind went into overdrive and my imagination got the better of me. However, my mind could not tell the difference between a twig or a real insect or rat on my leg because I couldn't see it. My mind had filled in the blanks and from my imagination I had created something that was going to bite me. There was nothing to be worried about, but my fight and fear response took over. I am sharing the funny story because it illustrates that when I am not normally scared of rats or spiders but I am not a big fan of snakes however in this situation because I couldn't see what was happening I reacted the way I did. Have a think when you may have been sacred or lost courage when something that was not a real threat, but your mind made it so. We will discuss more about the power of the mind later in this book.

5 second rule

"It's your moments of decision that your destiny is shaped" – Anthony Robbins

Consider reading an excellent book called "5 second rule" by Mell Robbins. This bestselling book focuses on the action habit and not the why or the motivation. The book looks at changing behavior and overcoming the negative habits. Counting down from five, four, three, two one then acting and overcoming procrastination. This effective and simple act can distract you from your negative thoughts. Whether it's getting up in the morning or going to work, going to the gym or applying for a new job. Researches have shown that half of the day we are on auto pilot which is a habit. Procrastinating is a habit so is self-doubt.

Action and behavior come from the thoughts that enter the Pre-fontal cortex so it's important to switching the gears in your mind with the right thoughts. If you want to learn to write with your non-dominant hand, then a new habit needs to be formed and this involves the reprogramming the frontal cortex. If you can learn to write and paint with your other hand that is if you are not naturally ambidextrous then think what other behaviors, you can change rather than the habit of pressing the snooze button. You just need to make a start you don't need to be super motivated to be successful and be brave and courageous. The 5 second rule was born from a television advert that the author saw of a rocket countdown to blast off. (10,9,8,7,6,5,4,3,2,1 blast off)

Five seconds is a shorter version of the rocket blast off and is a window of opportunity to overcome procrastination or the negative thoughts and feelings that can dominate. Researchers have found that 95% of decisions are made with feelings rather than logic. Do I feel like getting up or going to the gym no then you will not make it to the gym? These low feelings will be robbing you of joy and opportunity.

Malcolm Gladwell lay the foundation to the idea that you need 10,000 hours of practice to get good at anything, but these hours are made up of minutes and seconds. These important 5 seconds if acted on can make a real difference in your daily life.

Neuro Plastic Brain

Dr Lara Boyd Brain researcher from British Columbia found that when we learn something new, we change the brain it's called neuro plasticity. So, when we want to create new courageous habit this could be a temporary change or more permanent.

3 ways brain changes to support learning

1. More **chemical signals** created between neurons to support rapid short-term memory, so brain functions by transferring chemicals signals between brain cells, what we call neurons, and this triggers a series of actions and reactions. This kind of change can happen rapidly; this supports short term memory or the short-term improvement in the performance of a motor skill.

2. **Altering its structure** supports long term memory as neurons create new pathways such as learning to play a new instrument. So, during learning the brain can change the connections between neurons. Now here the physical structure of the brain is changing so this takes a bit more time. These types of changes are related to the long-term memory, the long-term improvement in a motor skill. You can't master guitar in one day as you quickly forget as only chemical changes have taken place. However, by repetition you lay down new neuron pathways and muscle memory. It's these physical changes that are now going to support long term memories, and chemical changes that support short term memories.

3. Functional changes

As you use a brain region it becomes more and more excitable and easy to use again so as your brain has these areas that increase their excitability. The brain shifts how and when they are activated. With learning we see that whole brain activity and network are shifting and changing.

By understanding how our brains learn we can start to master new habits and overcome fear and previously programmed behavior and have more courage.

When we experience fear our body reacts in a variety of ways.

What does fear, and anxiety feel like?

- Your muscles feel weak
- You feel frozen to the spot
- Your stomach churns or your bowels feel loose
- Your heart beats very fast – maybe it feels irregular
- You sweat a lot
- You can't eat

- You breathe very fast
- You find it hard to concentrate on anything else
- You feel dizzy
- You have hot and cold sweats
- You get a dry mouth
- You get very tense muscles

How to handle fear?

- Face your fears
- Recognize fear what triggers this fear, what do you avoid
- Embrace fear
- See fear as an opportunity, open the door to new opportunity
- Gradual exposure, acclimatizing
- Learn relaxation techniques, deep breathing, and mindfulness
- Educate yourself
- Have a plan to deal with it
- Visualize success
- Get help and seek advice

"Good medicine tastes bitter." Chinese proverb. Overcoming fear is a good medicine.

Chapter 2

CONFIDENCE: O for **OVERCOMING**

"Obstacles don't have to stop you. If you run into a wall, don't turn around and give up. Figure out how to climb it, go through it, or work around it."

These are the profound words from Michael Jordan the greatest basketball player of all time. We could all take on this advice from a super confident individual like Michael. Confident people like Michael portray certain number of traits one of which is the ability to overcome obstacles.

"When the wind of change blows, some build walls, while others build windmills." Chinese proverb.

Embrace change and obstacles, know that it's inevitable and the source of you becoming more confident.

If you think back to your own life you would have been faced with challenges and obstacles. These challenges are opportunities that test you out to see how you handle them and if your goal is important enough to you. All these circumstances change our lives to the better or worse. The obstacles that we have to overcome in life start as far back as our conception when 250million sperm have to compete to fertilize the egg and only around 400 will survive the 10hour journey to get there and then only one or more is able to complete its task. The growing egg develops into a fetus and then into a newborn baby over the next nine months. Then there is the miracle of birth and we are then nurtured through childhood, teenage years and before we become mature adults.

All through our life we make decisions of how to face these daily challenges. Some of these decisions turn out to be good for us and others not so good. However, if you decided to learn from these experiences so that they make you a more confident individual then that would have enriched your life. For some of you these obstacles, problems, challenges may have made you lose your confidence and you may have let these issues cut into the very fabric of your character. These same obstacles can even haunt you and cause physical and psychological restraints that hold you back from doing and achieving more with your abilities.

You may have had low confidence in certain areas of your life, and you may have then decided to seek out other things that you were better at and which didn't expose you to ridicule or embarrassment. However, avoiding these other new or unfamiliar activities would have had any effect on how you now behave. Think of what types of experiences have knocked your confidence and do you need to be revisited how this has impacted you. Sometimes it's up to you and how you reframe that experience to reshape a better you.

"Obstacles are those frightful things you see when you take your eyes off your goal." - Henry Ford

Let me ask you a few simple questions.

Did anyone make fun of you or ridiculed you while in school for asking questions in class?

The way you reacted to this experience as a child could have been why you rarely wanted to put your hands up to answer questions to avoid embarrassment.

Were you nervous when asked to speak in front of others that it literally made you ill?

When you tried a new sport or hobby in school or college were you quite hopeless so rather than improve you stopped to save yourself the embarrassment?

The answer to some of these questions will help you identify if fear and failure and personal embarrassment have held you back in those situations and did, they have a knock-on effect in other areas of your life. You may have avoided certain sports or other activities that exposed you to the possibility of embarrassment or perceived failure. This now became your avoidance strategy and new behavior.

For some people trying and failing in something new is too traumatic for them so they give up too easily so either move on to something else or it makes them warier of trying new things and soon fall into their comfort zones. The downside of this avoidance strategy is that you miss out on opportunities to learn new experiences in life, new careers new friendships and new love. You and I can have two different ways of looking at the same problem or situation. Do you leave problems and fears to fester and avoid dealing with them or do you put your solution hat on or game face on?

"It is not the problems that shape us in life but how we look at them and how we figure out what to do about them."

Gymnastics

Let's look at the sport of gymnastics where you usually start as a child and practice basic stretching, balancing and rolling skills before venturing into handstands, kart wheels and summersaults. Once some of these basic skills have become second nature then that child can be taught certain routines on the tumbling or floor work, Vault, beam and bars. Trampoline or safety pits are also used for training purposes. All gymnasts make mistakes from the beginner to the Olympic champions the difference between the beginner and the gold medalist is that the medalist has made a lot more mistakes then the beginner. The gold medalist has had many thousands of hours of practice over the years and they have fallen over many more times as well. However, their determination and hunger for success has spurned them on and they have not let the failures and mistakes along the way set them back.

For those of you old enough to remember let me take you back to 1996 Atlanta Olympics and the women's gymnastics event. There was a gymnast called Kerri Strug's. This young American gymnast was trying her best to gain points for her team while competing against the Russians. Kerri fell and had injured her ankle on her first attempt which meant that the American team had three falls in a row. She tried again after a painful first attempt. Her final vault she raised her game by being totally focused to win for the team, so she had to put the memory of the first fall behind her. The entire fate of the US teams now fell on her shoulders. Her vault was amazing, and the judges panel awarded 9.71 points which was enough for the USA to beat the Russians and to become the first American gymnastics team to take the gold medal. Even though Kerri unfortunately had to be carried off due to her ankle injury she will be remembered for her bravery and commitment to her team, country and sport.

Comfort zones

Any little obstacle whether it was mental or physical can create some early fear which may have affected your internal mindset that told you that if you keep doing this you will be disappointed, embarrassed and uncomfortable. This allowed you to the stay within your comfort zone that may have led you to do activities that caused you the least amount of stress. Each time we attempt something new or try and become better we test out the comfort zone boundaries and we need to break out of these boundaries in order to grow. Some people start to venture out of their comfort zones but soon return because it was too challenging to overcome the obstacles or others have ridicule them for trying to improve their circumstances. In order to grow we must form the habit of overcoming obstacles and exploring outside of our comfort zones. This is when we have the biggest results and break through.

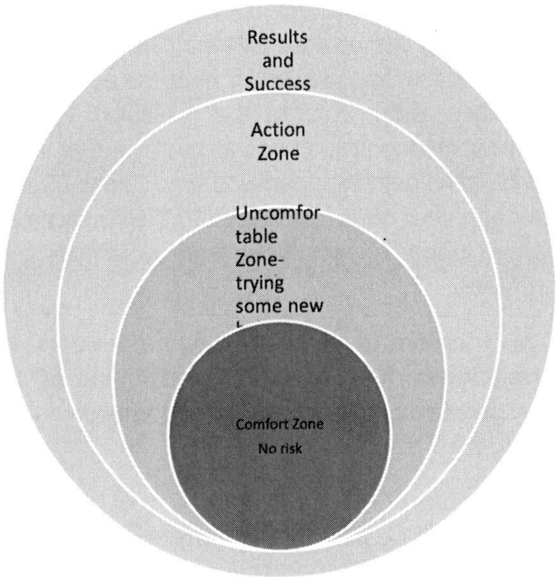

You may have even had some initial success in your life and then some incident triggered a massive loss in confidence. This could be a breakup of relationship, a business failing, a loss of someone close to you or being made redundant or failing a test. Whatever the trigger was it may have knocked you off your normal game in life that led to a low period or even depression may have even set in. You may have even turned to self-neglect to drink or drugs overstaying late at work with no care for your health or family and friends. All these activities have been detrimental to your wellbeing. Was there someone around you at the time that was there to help and support you if so, did you talk through your issues and listen to their advice or ignore it and consume your self in your own troubles?

This incident in your life may have been the trigger that led you to certain set of circumstances that you are no longer happy with.

Are you one of those people that allow obstacles to knock your confidence and make you weaker or are you one that gets their confidence knocked but is prepared to get back and face whatever challenge faces you. Obstacles are there throughout your life and they are there to test you and by facing them head on and overcoming them each day will make you stronger when you finally reach your goal. I know it's not easy but most good things in life never is.

If we look at the timeline below its shows that obstacles can knock your confidence and self-esteem, or you can bounce back and become stronger.

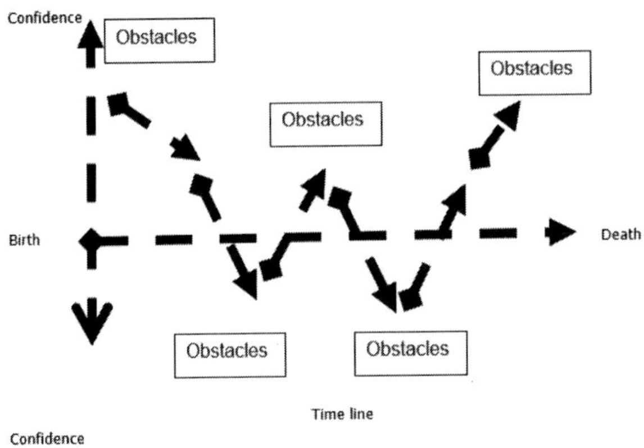

Obstacles are usually only temporary since it is not always possible to change what has happened, but we can change the way we look at it.

"When you climb to the top of the obstacle that is blocking your view, you are able to look at your situation from a different perspective."- Lucy MacDonald

How do we now turn around these fears and concerns so that we can become more confident and powerful rather than powerless? Well it would be a good idea to analyze or even categories these fears and concerns so that we have better understanding. This way we can come up with a way of tackling them.

Let me ask you these 7 power questions. The power comes from writing them down since the brain starts going into solution mode. This is providing that you have the conviction and perseverance to tackle these obstacles in a can-do attitude.

Ask these 7 questions to yourself but imagine you are a character such as a detective from your favorite TV program. You could be Sherlock Holmes, Mrs. Marple or Precious Ramotswe

Botswana's only female detective Colombo. Now have you chosen a character to play well then that's great. If not, then have a think again before progressing to answer these next 7 questions.

You are now actually going to play two characters one is the victim of the crime that we now call 'obstacle' the other character is the detective you have chosen to be who is asking the question to solve the crime.

Here are the questions

1.Do you know what caused you to lose confidence?
2.Do you understand how it is affecting you?
3.Can you live with the obstacle or does your attitude and approach need to change towards it?
4.Do you have the skills to deal with this obstacle or do need to you seek expert advice?
5.Can you come back to dealing with the obstacle after a good night sleep?
6.Have you been shown courage to overcome the obstacle or have you not tapped into this power?

7.Is the real obstacle you? If this is the case how do you need to change?

By answering these questions honestly and writing them down it will be liberating. By pretending to a being in character of your chosen detective then this will help you to look at your obstacle in a whole new perspective and through the eyes and viewpoint of the detective that you most admire. Work with the answers and you can come up with a solution that is going to work for you.

Well now that you have answered the 7 questions that you had asked yourself you should be 7 steps closer to working out your own solution. Another option is to work closely with a kind and considerate friend or family member who is none judgmental that you can confide in then meet with them to discuss your answers since they may be part of the solution. There will be many occasions in your life when you will have to overcome obstacles. Whether this obstacle is coming to terms with your current challenges or having the confidence to overcome future hurdles. You can not dwell on your situation you have to look for solutions.

Plan and find the power within to deal with these emotions so that you can overcome them.

"What do you mean aren't you going to give me any answers" I hear you say.

Think again did you find this book from the self-help and personal development section or was it in "Give me the answers section because I am not prepared to work them out myself"

Let's be brutally honest you picked this book to try and help and possibly inspire you well that's great. From over 30 years of coaching people in leadership, life coaching and in martial arts I have come across some individuals that want a quick fix to make them better faster and stronger, yet it took most of their life to end up with the problems they have. I can lead you to the door of knowledge it's up to you to open it and absorb all you can, and only then will your own mind come up with the answers. These answers are then your answers and not one that has been bought off the self. Therefore, so many people start on a new fad diet and lose weight only to gain it back again 6 to 12 months later. The quick fix answer off the self is not the way forward. I truly believe that all human beings have the answers to their most of life's problems and obstacles.

"It's only when the student is ready that the teacher can teach, that student is you and that teacher is you."

This book is just a conduit to helping you as a student to ready your body and mind to a better way of solving life's problems.

Are we now ready to move on or have you stopped reading and have already thrown the book away?

For those of you still reading let's get back to ways of handling the obstacle. Firstly, you need to identify what the obstacle is before you can overcome it. It is easier if you simplify them and then you can proceed to conquer the obstacle. We all choose how to handle situations differently and we need to be comfortable with the one we choose. There will be many choices that you have in life so it's worth knowing a way to handle whatever life throws at you.

In life we all experience tough times, so remember you are not alone. Tough times are there for us to better ourselves and become a stronger person. Remember **tough times never last but tough people do**. If you have a strong enough will power and you tell yourself you can do it, and then we can overcome any obstacle that life throws at us.

"If you can find a path with no obstacles, it probably doesn't lead anywhere." - Frank A. Clark

You may have heard the words from the Billy Ocean song

"When the going gets tough the tough get going"

Well now it's your turn to get tough.

Have an action plan to make sure that you can overcome potential pitfalls and obstacles.

Plan 6 Ps

Proper

Planning

Prevents

Particularly

Poor

Performance

Always have a plan B, C, or D ... if plan A doesn't work. This chapter is not about planning however it's like the words below uttered by the Cheshire cat.

"If you don't know where you're going, any road will take you there" was essentially a paraphrase of an exchange between Alice and the Cheshire cat in Chapter 6 of Lewis Carroll's Alice's Adventures in Wonderland: "Would you tell me, please, which way I ought to go from here?"

You need to know where you want to go.

To plan to overcome your obstacle and pursue a goal for your life you will need to know -

- Where you want to go?
- Why you want to get there?
- What are you prepared to do to get there?
- How are you going to get there?
- When do you want to get there by?

Answering these questions will help you plan how to overcome your obstacle.

It's also important to have a C-SMART goal.

What Does C- SMARTER Mean?

C- SMART is an acronym that you can use to guide your goal setting.

This is attributed to Peter Drucker's Management by Objectives concept. The first known use of the term occurs in the November 1981 issue of Management Review by George T. Doran. Since then, Professor Robert S. Rubin (Saint Louis University) wrote about SMART in an article for The Society for Industrial and Organizational Psychology. He stated that SMART has come to mean different things to different people, as shown below.

Some useful tips to make sure your goals are clear and reachable:

- **C-Challenging**

- **S-Specific** (simple, sensible, significant).

- **M-Measurable** (meaningful, motivating).
- **A-Achievable** (agreed, attainable).
- **R-Relevant** (reasonable, realistic and resourced, results-based).
- **T-Time bound** (time-based, time limited, time/cost limited, timely, time-sensitive).
- **E-Evaluated** and
- **R-Reviewed**

Professor Rubin also notes that the definition of the SMART acronym may need updating to reflect the importance of efficacy and feedback. However, some authors have expanded it to include extra focus areas.

When you are at your lowest and you are least confident is at this point when life is testing you. Throughout these tough periods you need to believe in yourself, be persistent, remain calm, and get additional support from friends and family. You must be realistic and see the obstacle for what it really is.

Are you making the obstacle bigger than what it is and making a mountain out of a molehill?

Think about how you could turn the obstacle into a positive, so look for hidden opportunities. If you keep a positive outlook and view the obstacle in a positive way instead of a negative way, you will overcome the obstacle a lot quicker. This may mean that you must change your thought process but by doing this it will help you make positives out of negatives situations in life.

If you consider obstacles as danger, then they can also be opportunities and stepping-stones.

The word NO spelt backwards is ON. So, you can turn things around when faced with no's and rejections in your life.

NO/ON

In the Chinese language, the word "crisis" has its origins from two characters, one representing danger and the other, opportunity. So, you too can learn from facing crisis and turn them into opportunities to grow.

"Patience and perseverance have a magical effect before which difficulties disappear and obstacles vanish." - John Quincy Adams

Learn from the past

Think back to how you overcame small obstacles in your life. How can you apply what you have learnt to your current circumstances?

We learn to become stronger by testing our minds and bodies to overcome obstacles. Obstacle can be a source of frustration and pain. Obstacles and challenges can be a source of excitement, satisfaction and fulfillment. Decide that behind every Obstacle there is an answer and you will be surprised what solutions will appear. You decide that you are in control your life and not obstacles that hold you back. Always look harder and deeper after facing hurdles or obstacles and be patient to wait to see the opportunities.

Thomas Edison is said to have tried 10,000 times before perfecting the light bulb

"I have not failed. I've just found 10,000 ways that won't work." -Thomas Edison.

Edison was famous for never giving up in his search for the construction of the electric light bulb. Without his tenacity and almost hard-headed way of never giving up, his idea may not have ever come to fruition.

Helen Keller was an American author, political activist and lecturer who was deaf and blind once said, **"Life is a daring adventure, or nothing."**

Obstacles are the essence of your daring adventure, so embrace them and their solutions

Boulders can be obstacles in your way or stepping-stones to a better life.

Milala Yousafzai a Pakistani female activist and youngest noble prize laureate who made a miraculous recovery from an assassination attempt on her life by the Taliban who shot her in the head.

"When the whole world is silent even one voice becomes powerful." - Milala Yousafzai

If Milala can recover from the obstacles she had to face you can use your one inner voice to become your power to change.

Accept that you will have obstacles to deal with all your life. Most people that are confident are surprisingly the ones that have faced the most adversity and yet have lived and learnt from it. They have come out the other side of adversity to become better and stronger individuals.

Greta Thunberg – A Swedish female climate activist who also has autism, whose mission is to get politicians and all people to wake up to save our planet from self-destruction.

"I don't want your hope. I want you to panic. I want you to act. I want you to feel the fear I feel every day. I want you to act as you would in a crisis. I want you to act as if your house is on fire, because it is." - Greta Thunberg

In other words, is your personal life on Fire, act now before it's too late.

It's your time no to overcome the obstacles in your life.

Chapter 3

CO**N**FIDENCE: N for **Negativity**

"Positive thinking will let you do everything better than negative thinking will!" - Zig Ziglar

Frog story

Drawings by Chandni Soren

Let us revisit Jabari and Diallo from the first chapter. The African Grandfather related a story to the young boy about the importance of having a positive outlook on life. He told the story about two frogs one called

Phomello means **to succeed** and he is the positive frog the other frog called

Naggad means **to be a critic** reviewer and is the negative frog.

Jabari goes on to relate the story about two frogs one called **Phomello** the **Positive** and optimistic frog and **Naggad** the **Negative** and pessimistic frog.

These two frogs were out one day looking for something to eat.

The Positive frog kept saying "I am sure that we are going to find something nice to eat". While Negative frog kept saying "Oh it's too hot and we will never find anything nice to eat"

They searched and searched all day until they finally came across a milk urn.

Phomello said "let's jump inside and see. I am sure that it will be good."

Naggad said "No it's probably got a snake in it or some giant spider."

Phomello said "don't worry just be positive"

They both jumped in and found themselves in a vat of milk.

Naggad said. "I told you there was no food in here plus we are going to drown in milk."

Phomello- "Don't worry. We will get out just wait and see."

They both tried to jump out of the milk urn but to no avail.

Phomello said "Just keep on paddling something will turn up."

Naggad said "What is the use of paddling it's not going to achieve anything plus I am getting tired."

Phomello said "Just keeping on paddling"

They paddled but the negative frog soon got disheartened.

Naggad said "I am not going to paddle any longer. I think it's a waste of time, so he soon stopped paddling and then sank to the bottom of the milk and soon died."

Nothing that Phomello said could dissuade Naggad from sinking to the bottom. Phomello even tried to hold Naggad above the milk but Naggad let go and sank to his death.

Phomello was a sad to see Naggad sink to the bottom.

Phomello soon got his thoughts back on track and kept on paddling and paddling. After several hours of paddling the milk became thicker and the heat of sun made it even thicker.

Soon the milk began to curdle then it became cream and then a few hours later it became butter.

Soon the butter attracted flies which Phomello feasted on.

Since the butter was hard it allowed him to jump out of the urn and go home to his family with an extra supply of flies, but he had to inform others about the loss of Naggad.

There are several morals of this story

- Stay positive and optimistic even under the most difficult circumstances.

- Actions do not initially produce results so have faith to keep on doing some action until you get the desired outcome.

- Don't hang around negative people or take their advice they can keep you from achieving your goals.

- If **we think** we can, we can. If we think we can't then **we can't?**

- Success **comes in 'cans' and not in can nots.**

- Your attitude and actions can shape your future for the better or worse.

Be positive and act and the opportunities will present themselves. The opposite of negative thinking is obviously Positive Thinking. If you remember back to the story of Jabari and Diallo the grandson asks the question who would win in a fight the lion or the hyena? The answer he gave was: "The one that would win is the one who is the stronger in heart, body and mind"

Even though the lion should always win in a one to one battle the grandfather said the hyena could win if the lion doubted itself. This all relates to Positive thinking since it is a way of looking at any circumstance and finding the good in it. It could take 10 or more positive thoughts to overcome powerful negative thoughts. So, you may need to saturate your mind with positive thoughts that you believe in.

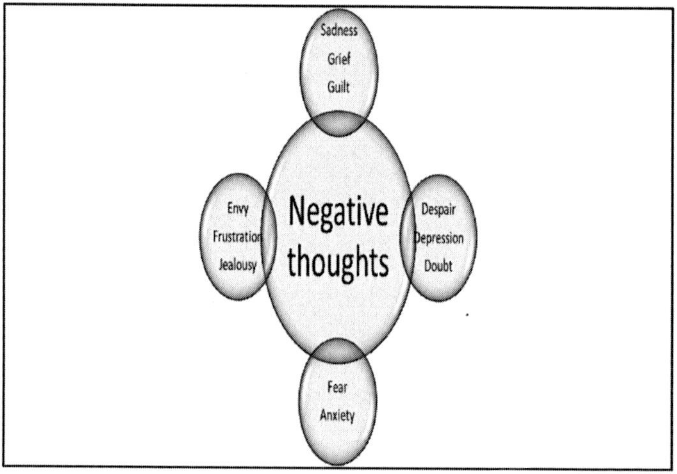

Negative thoughts and emotions may include several feeling and emotions.

- Doubt
- Despair
- Envy
- Depression
- Guilt
- Shame
- Grief
- Sadness
- Envy
- Anger
- Jealousy
- Frustration

Ask yourself a few more questions.

When you look at the world around you,

- Do you see the glass half full or half empty?

- Do you have problems or are they challenges?
- Do you always see the worst in a situation, or can you see what good can come out of it?

The answers that you gave should be a small indication as to how you naturally think. However, it's totally normal to have negative feelings since it makes us human.

Titanic mind

Thomas Andrews's ship designer assured everyone that the Titanic was unsinkable, Captain E.J. Smith ignored the Ice berg warnings, and Bruce Ismay the director of the cruise was convinced that they had to proceed at speed to arrive in New York in 6 days as promised to his passengers. Stanley Lord was the captain of the California which initially sent out the iceberg warning but turned off their radios thinking that the Titanic was safe and that the flares emanating from the Titanic were celebratory fireworks. The shipbuilders were confident that they had built the unsinkable ship but many of the 3 million rivets used were of poor quality and were substandard iron. There were also not enough lifeboats on board to carry all the passengers because the ship was thought to be unsinkable.

If we can imagine that for some people that their minds are like the Titanic engineer and the negative thoughts and comments are like the iceberg. The job of this Titanic mind is to avoid sinking yet it may not have fully prepared for its voyage of life on the treacherous seas.

- This type of mind may not have prepared for all eventualities and challenges that were to be faced on this voyage.

- This mind may not have been stress tested to see it could handle unexpected occurrences.

- This mind may not have the fortitude and resilience and map reading skills to avoid possible tragic outcomes.

If the mind is arrogant obsessed with in its own self-importance, then it does not see the whole picture. The mind needs to be open minded enough to explore in detail warnings signs and how to deal with worse case scenarios. These people may not have a backup plan in life and work at full speed until they eventually drop dead of a heart attack or their relationships fail with family friends and work colleagues. This is like the titanic not having enough lifeboats as a backup plan. It's like the Titanic having substandard rivets or only having 16 watertight chambers to save on passenger space rather than provide better safety precautions. So how does this all relate to the Titanic mind well let's think this through. We may know someone that abuses their bodies and minds my taking in drugs and excessive alcohol or other things. They may have been warned by others round them as well as experts that this type of habit is going to be their downfall if they continue this course. This is like the iceberg warning given to the Titanic and to reduce the speed of the ship when approaching such waters renowned for icebergs, but the ships designer thought the ship was unsinkable and asked the captain to sail through the icebergs.

There are other individuals that may have had daily diet and brain washing of negativity such as racism and evil ideologies. Well by taking this poisonous diet it can only make the mind eviler, self-destructive and over-confident. This type of negative diet is going to corrupt the mind and cracks are going to show people are getting to get hurt around them and as we know when this type of mind is eventually stopped, or it hits something as hard as massive iceberg the result is catastrophic.

I am sure that we all wish to avoid this type of Titanic mindset so it's worth making sure that the diet we feed our minds is balanced and buoyant in order that we can stay afloat no matter how rough the seas become.

How are you with mathematics?

Here's a little challenge for you: -

This is a small exercise for you to try out so make sure you have a pen and paper at hand. Have you found a pen and paper that's great?

Write this down

1x1=2

2x2=4

3x3=10

4x4=16

LITTLE POCKET OF CONFIDENCE

5x5=25

Look at the sums and see if you can you spot anything about the answers?

Some of you would say I have spotted one wrong answer or there were 4 correct answers and one incorrect?

If this was mathematics test you would have got a straight A with a pass mark of 80%.

However, many people only see the wrong answer and when we view others sometimes, we only see the bad in them or in ourselves. Sometimes we have a blind spot and cannot see what things are good in others and ourselves so only focus on the bad and negative.

Positive thinking can be as simple as seeing the 4 correct answers and the good in others.

Our thoughts work in a cycle, all action begins with a thought and if we add emotion to it, you will begin to act on it, if we repeat this action often enough, it will become a habit, and if you keep doing this habit, it will become a part of your character. As human beings we can almost be seen just as individuals who are made up of a series of habits! I realize that we are more complicated than this but it's one way of trying to simplify things to get the idea across.

The Scorpion and the Frog

Drawing by Chandni Soren

The earliest known publication of this fable was in the 1944 book The Hunter of the Pamirs: A

LITTLE POCKET OF CONFIDENCE

Novel of Adventure in Soviet Central Asia by Georgi Tushkan. It was made famous by the 1955 film Mr. Arkadin and 'The Crying Game'

One day, a scorpion was not happy with where he lived and decided that he wanted a change. So, he set out on a journey. He kept climbing over rocks and kept going until he reached a river.

The river was wide and fast running, and the scorpion stopped to reconsider the situation. It couldn't see any way across. So, it ran upriver and downriver, all the while thinking that it might have to turn back.

Suddenly, he saw a frog sitting in the bushes by the bank of the river. He asked the frog to help him get across the stream.

"Hello Mr. Frog!" called the scorpion, "Would you be so kind as to give me a ride on your back across the river?"

"Well now, Mr. Scorpion! How do I know that if I try to help you, you won't try to kill me?" asked the hesitant frog.

"Because," the scorpion replied, "If I try to kill you, then I would die too, and I cannot swim! I will protect you from the frog eating stalk bird on the other side".

Now this seemed to make sense to the frog. But he asked. "What about when I get close to the other side? You could still try to kill me and jump to the shore!"

"This is true," agreed the scorpion, "But then I wouldn't be able to get to the other side!"

"Alright then...how will I know that you won't just wait till we get to the other side and then you will kill me?" said the frog.

"Well," the scorpion said, "Because I give you my word once you've taken me to the other side of this river, I will be so grateful for your help, that it would not be fair of me kill you, now would it?!"

So, the frog agreed to take the scorpion across the river and picked up his passenger. The scorpion crawled onto the frog's back. The water splashed around them, but the frog stayed near the surface, so the scorpion would not drown.

Halfway across the river, the frog suddenly felt a sharp sting in his back and, out of the corner of his eye, saw the scorpion remove his stinger from the frog's back. A numbness began to creep into his limbs which would soon kill him.

"You fool!" croaked the frog, "Now we shall both die! Why did you do that?"

The scorpion shrugged.

"I could not help myself. It is my nature."

Then they both sank into the water and died, and the stalk feasted on them both.

What a story of self-destruction - "It's my Nature", said the Scorpion...

Well what can we learn from this fable?

Can we learn not to trust certain people as they are like the scorpion and it's in their nature to be negative and evil? Don't be fooled by some people that make promises.

Hopefully you are not the scorpion however we may have the seeds of nature of self-destruction or self-sabotage and sit in our comfort zone rather than take the risk to succeed.

Chapter 4

CONFIDENCE - F for **FEELINGS**

"One looks back with appreciation to the brilliant teachers, but with gratitude to those who touched our human feeling. The curriculum is so much necessary raw material, but warmth is the vital element for the growing plant and for the soul of a child." Carl Jung

Feelings are a very important part of our human make up and it's an emotional state and reaction to events and thoughts. We experience them every second of the day. Feelings can be our allies or traitors depending on our ability to harness them. If they get out of balance and can lead to emotional overdrive.

There are many types of feelings and emotions that stir us and can help us achieve our goals to greater confidence

Exercise

Have a look at the list below and tick the emotions and feelings that dominate your daily life. If you are experiencing more negative feelings and emotions as indicated on the right-hand list below then you will need to make some serious changes to improve your circumstances. You may even need to seek professional medical advice if you only have negative feelings most of the time. There are a lot more feelings and emotions that we experience so this is not an exhaustive list.

Feelings	Tick	Feelings	Tick
Joy		Sadness	
Love		Anger	
Serenity		Jealousy	

Hope		Shame	
Gratitude		Embarrassment	
Serenity		Ignored	
Enthusiasm		Humiliated	
Interest		Criticized	
Satisfaction		Inferior	
Inspiration		Mocked	
Kindness		Worthless	
Pride		Invisible	
Confidence		Confused	
Cheerfulness		Cynical	
Admiration		Skeptical	
Accepted		Worthless	
Valued		Rejected	

Thoughts Actions Habits Character Cycle

Thinking positively about a situation is just a habit. It is something we can develop and something we can control. Whatever circumstances are thrown at us, whatever situations we face, we can always choose how we think and feel about the situation. We can choose to wallow in self-pity or find what good there is in the situation.

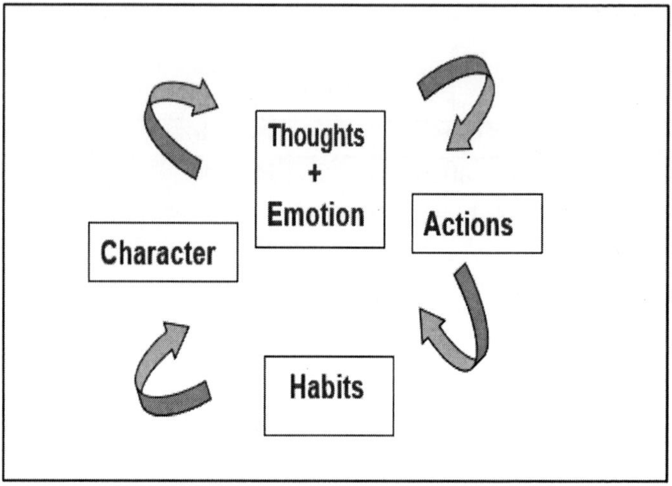

"You are the only one who can control the way you think. Make sure you nourish the positive thoughts and weed out the negative ones!" - Catherine Pulsifer.

If you are having problems/ challenges in your life now, what good can you see in this situation?

It could do with:

- Lack of money
- Poor health
- No job
- Few friends
- No support
- Dealing with an addiction
- Poor relationships
- Debts
- Depressed or other mental health issues please seek professional help.

Yes, it can be hard to deal with these things however it's about your **positive attitude and thinking, self-belief** towards these things that will determine the outcome.

Think of the **SOLUTION** and not the **PROBLEM and your feelings and thoughts will improve**

Others have had the same challenges as listed above however they have overcome them.

Plan and prepare for better feelings and emotions life. Try taking small steps to success and planning and things will improve for you over time.

"By the yard it's hard, but inch by inch anything is a cinch." Brian Tracy

"Each day in every way I am getting better and better" Coined by a Frenchman named Emile Coue

You may be thinking, all well and good, but what about me?

How can my situation be seen in a good light?

Looking at it in another way just think about your own personal experiences you have been through, what would you do if you had to do it again? You might not be able to change your choices, but do you think they may be another person like yourself, going through a similar situation? Maybe you could share your experiences with them and help them make a more informed choice.

"Work joyfully and peacefully, knowing that right thoughts and right efforts will inevitably bring about right results." - James Allen

How can we train ourselves to practice positive and productive feelings and good thinking and emotions?

Here are few useful tips

- Visualize your success
- Every time you have a negative emotion, replace it with a positive one
- Don't build up obstacles, see them for what they are
- Don't compare yourself to other people, you are doing the best you can under the circumstance you have.
- Have a positive dialogue about yourself
- Get help from someone who can help you understand yourself.
- Make a list of things that you are thankful for and have achieved in your life to date.

Peter Pan

Think of Disney character Peter Pan who always remained a boy and who could fly when he had happy thoughts. This story of Peter Pan was inspired by a tragedy. The Scottish play write and novelist J.M Barrie was inspired to write even though he had faced personal tragedy. His older brother died in an ice-skating accident the day before he had turned 14. Thus, he always stayed a boy. J.M. Barrie used his experience to share many wonderful stories and plays and one that many of us know as Peter Pan. Just think the same is true for you and me when we have happy positive up lifting thoughts then you too can feel that you can conquer the world and achieve great things.

In Mary Poppins movie when the characters were laughing when drinking a cup of tea, they started to float up in the air. Happy funny thoughts made them fly.

In real life we cannot float in the air unless we are in space however we can feel like we are floating and flying away to better place in our mind and thoughts in order to take the actions we need by having happier and more positive thoughts.

Tips to better harness your feelings and emotions

- Be good at recognizing your own emotions and those of others
- Learn to be a good listener
- Learn to read other people's emotions from their body language and what they say or not say
- Learn to be more patient.
- Learn to disagree with others in a respectful manner without being too emotional
- Compliment others more often rather then look for the negative
- Find a calm place to relax and have some down time.

Try making a note of what feelings you are experiencing when your confidence is high and improving and when it is taking a knock. Is it a certain situation or person that makes you feel more confident or less confident? Once you know this then you are in a better position to tackle it. It is going to take work on your behalf to tame these emotions and feelings so stick at it and then you will eventually succeed.

Decide each day that you are better at expressing good feelings and emotions. Spend time with people that bring about good feelings and invest in activities that add to your positive emotions. It doesn't mean that we only spend time in a happy place and situations as each day we face a whole range of emotions which can either bring us to our knees and make us cry or angry or lift us up and feel like we can achieve anything. Become a feeling and emotions champion as well as an expert but this only comes over time and experience and facing whatever life throws at you. This way you can make small steps to better confidence later leading to big strides.

Chapter 5

CONF**I**DENCE: I is for **INSPIRATION**

"Inspiration comes from making connections, from seeing beautiful new things. Inspiration really is, for me, a constant state. Inspiration comes from being alive." -Tony Buzan

Just take a moment to think about what inspires you in your everyday life. Many things can inspire you such as individuals that you respect and admire. You may be inspired by dreams and ambitions that drive you forward. You may be inspired by your religion or humanitarian causes and to make the world a better place. People can inspire you and you can also inspire others.

Whether this person is famous or a close friend or relative or even a stranger, they can inspire you in many ways and help shape your actions, behavior and beliefs. You can inspire others whether they are friends or family. If you are a parent, you can inspire children and other parents. If you are in a job or business, you too can inspire those around you.

Inspire or expire

"Some people in life are inspired to take action while there are those without dreams and hopes and instead become expired."

Think about what will inspire you and keep you motivated to achieve more out of your life. The more you are inspired the more confidence will grow and you will be able to overcome many of those of fears that have held you back. You will grow in mind body and spirit when you become inspired with passion to overcome what situations come your way.

"It's not only children who grow parents do too. As much as we watch to see what our children do with their lives, they are watching us to see what we do with ours.

I can't tell my children to reach for the sun. All I can do is reach for it myself."
Joyce Maynard

Achieving new things in your life will inspire those around you as well as you. If those around you always see you as being lazy or being afraid to try new things, then what impression would that leave with them. Would you be a good role model to others if not then aim to be one by starting with the simplest things?

- It might be as simple as being the first person to smile in the office and saying hello.

- It might be making sure that you encourage and congratulate others around you for doing good things at work or at home.

- It might be to offer to help others raise money for charity and take part in the activity with them.

- Start to read inspirational stories a book's such as '**Chicken soup for the sou**l' by Jack Canfield and Mark Victor Hansen

If you start to help others with inspiring ventures and ideas then you too will be inspired to do more, be more active, have more fun and achieve more. Read and find out about people as much as you can that inspire you. Read inspirational stories that move you and bring tears to your eyes and warm your heart and soul. These types of activities enrich your life and slowly but surely works on your internal psyche to say yes. I too can change and have better and more confident life.

If you cannot find role models around, you then you become the new role model that can inspire those around you. One of the things I have done to inspire others is that I have used my skills as a Ju Jitsu and Aikido instructor to inspire children and adults that they too can master a new skill. This could be to learn a new arm lock a throw or a new way of defending yourself from an assailant. I have taught many thousands of children and adults over the last 36 years and have seen their confidence grow. I was also nervous and had low confidence when I first started to learn Ju jitsu but slowly but surely I started to improve and had knock backs along the way and had had broken ribs, broken

> shoulder blade as part of my training and at one point almost lost an eye. This knocked my confidence at first, but I had to believe in my -self again and to gain the courage to back into the dojo (training room) and rebuild my confidence. Like anything new in life, it begins by being brave enough to take the first step into a dojo and week by week a new student learns new moves and techniques and make mistakes along the way. These same students then overcome their fear by entering their first grading and they can show the Sensei what they have learnt.

The student's ordeal is finally over after one or two hours and they are delighted to hear those wonderful words "**Well done you have passed, and you are now a yellow belt**" The students then have beaming smiles that last for a week or more and some children will go home and have their photographs taken and post their success to the world on social media. Some children are so proud that they even sleep wearing their new yellow belt. This ritual of training and grading continues its cycle through each of their first few gradings from yellow belt orange belt and all the way to brown then their black belt. As part of their journey the student then starts to inspire others around them, and they become the new role models.

Does this mean that you to have to become a black belt in Ju Jitsu or aikido or other martial art not unless you want to but at least try and become the best role model that you can be for your family, for your community for your work and for your business. Inspired people can change the world for the better. Make your life better by discovering what excites and really inspires you. Once you have latched on to a truly inspirational idea or thought then hold on to it with your life and make the best of it for you and those around you.

To learn more about martial arts such as Ju Jitsu or Aikido look on the internet or go to www.jitsufoundation.org , www.aikiflow.uk www.takemusu.org and www.bradfordjitsu.org.uk .

"**Accept responsibility for your life. Know that it is you who will get you where you want to go, no one else."**-Brian Tracy

Take some time now to read to some truly inspirational life stories. The first one is about someone who had overcome immense physical obstacles to become the person he now is.

Nick Vujicic

Nick was born in Melbourne, Australia with the rare Tetra-amelia disorder. This meant that he was missing both arms at shoulder level and having one small foot with two toes protruding from his left thigh. Despite all these challenges and the absence of limbs, he is happy and living life without limits. He surfs and swims and plays golf and soccer. Nick graduated from college at the age of 21 with a double major in Accounting and Financial Planning. He now travels as a motivational speaker, focusing on the topics that today's teenager's face. I was truly moved by his story and how he mastered his limb disorder and is living a fulfilling life. I am sure you too will be moved and inspired by what Nick has to say so make the time and effort to look him up on YouTube.

J. K. Rowling

Take another inspiring yet different example of J.K. Rowling's who we know as the author of

Harry Potter. Her first marriage ended in divorce and this was to a Portuguese television journalist. She then moved near her sister in Edinburgh with her baby daughter where she had to initially live on government welfare benefits. She lived in a rundown apartment which was infested with mice and was then also clinically diagnosed with depression. She drew on this for her books when she introduced the dementors. She spent time writing Harry Potter but was initially rejected by at least 12 publishers. A year later she was delighted to get an £1500 advance by Editor Barry Cunningham from Bloomsbury, a small publishing house in London. Alice Newton an eight-year-old who was the daughter of Bloomsbury's chairman initially reviewed the first chapter and demanded the next one. Cunningham was reported to have advised Rowling to get a day job, since she had little chance of making money in children's books. We of course all know that she never got the day job since in 1997, Rowling received an £8000 grant from the Scottish Arts Council to enable her to continue writing. Over the next 20 years she became a world-famous author selling over 400 million books and becoming one of the richest and influential women of recent times and estimated Harry Potter brand worth of over $15 billion.

In June 2008 JK Rowling delivered the commencement address below at Harvard University.

"Failure meant a stripping away of the inessential. I stopped pretending to myself that I was anything other than what I was and began to direct all my energy to finishing the only work that mattered to me. Had I really succeeded at anything else, I might never have found the determination to succeed in the one area where I truly belonged. I was set free, because my greatest fear had been realized, and I was still alive, and I still had a daughter whom I adored, and I had an old typewriter, and a big idea. And so rock bottom became a solid foundation on which I rebuilt my life."

This is one example of someone who faced depression and turned her life around in massive way.

The Beatles

In 1962, an executive of Decca Records made the following statement about a singing group: "We don't like their sound. Besides, groups playing guitars are on the way out anyway." He was talking about the Beatles.

Jack Canfield and Mark Victor Hansen

Jack Canfield and Mark Victor Hansen, co-authors of the world renowned "Chicken Soup for the Soul" book series, were turned down by 33 of New York's biggest publishing houses in the first month.

They were told "We don't think there is a market for this book." "We just don't get it." "The book is too positive." In total they were rejected by 140 publishers and even their agent said, "I can't sell this book — I'm giving it back to you guys."

They finally found someone by the name of Peter Vegso, President of Health Communications, Inc who was willing to invest in their book. The first books were published on June 28, 1993 and had become a favorite by the end of December and these series of books sold over 60 million copies. To top this Jack and Mark are featured The Guinness Book of World Records for having the most books on the New York Times bestseller list at one time; seven books on May 24, 1998.

If you are still unsure about how others in life have overcome their own obstacles look at these highly successful people overcame to reach their goals.

Abraham Lincoln lost 12 major elections before he finally gained presidency of the United States of America.

Ludwig van Beethoven triumphed over both a hearing loss and early discouragement from his music teacher who said that 'as a composer, he was hopeless,' yet he went on to become one of the most famous composers of classical music.

Martin Luther King, Marie Curie, Nelson Mandela, Emily Pankhurst, Mahatma Gandhi inspired a nations and millions of people of their generation and around the world.

Who will you inspire?

Be inspired yourself before you can inspire others.

The reason that these people eventually reached their goals was because they refused to give up, no matter how many difficulties they encountered, and how little faith other people had in them. They kept their faith in themselves, and ultimately their courage and persistence paid off. They were inspired by those around them and they too have become inspirational.

Each time you are moved by an inspirational story use this emotion as fuel to inspire you to tackle that thing that's been holding you back from doing what must be done to help you on your confidence journey.

"We are more than 'human beings' we define our lives by those things that we do for others in society so become a 'human doing' and leave a legacy for others to follow in your footsteps."

Chapter 6

CONFI**D**ENCE: D for **DETERMINATION**

"We all have dreams. But in order to make dreams come into reality. it takes an awful lot of determination, dedication, self-discipline, and effort." – Jesse Owens

A person who exhibits abundant confidence is someone who has determination, drive, self-discipline and a single-minded approach to getting things done.

You are probably familiar with the saying.
"Where there is will there is a way"

Determination is a firmness of purpose or resoluteness. Specifically, being determined means having a firm decision or goal and not wavering in your pursuit of achieving it. An athlete might have a goal to finish a marathon race and their determination gives them the motivation to wake up early to train, push on through the race and to keep moving forward when they are feeling tired and exhausted. Determination in business or the workplace manifests differently than determination in athletics, but it is just as important.

What makes a determined person?

- The Determined don't give up on their goal,
- The Determined don't let failure stop them.
- The Determined don't require the approval of others.

- The Determined don't fear rejection.
- The Determined don't let limiting beliefs stop them from moving forward.
- The Determined don't let the fear of failure stop them
- The Determined don't let what they don't know stop them.
- Determined People don't shy away from challenges

What are the benefits of determination?

- Determination spurs creativity
- Determination gives you hope
- Determination helps you motivate others
- Determination provides guidance and motivation
- Determination pushes you to go above and beyond others

Action

- Set yourself small and achievable goals
- Have a deep belief in your goal
- Do not complain about your circumstances but look for solutions
- Stay focused and avoid distraction

Types of motivation

Extrinsic motivation: When you are motivated to act by external factors, such as rewards by more pay or compensation or praise.

Intrinsic motivation: Intrinsic motivation is when you feel inspired to complete a task because it aligns with your personal core values.

Fear Motivation: The fear of negative consequences can drive you to avoid an unpleasant experience such as not paying the tax bill or fear of being made redundant.

Achievement motivation: This motivation involves having to perform tasks to achieve specific objectives.

Affiliation motivation: Also known as social motivation, this motivation encourages social interaction among people.

Power motivation: When you spend hundreds of hours to build your own business or become an expert in your field, you are trying to gain control over your livelihood.

Attitude motivation: This is the motivation that drives an individual to change other people's perception or thoughts.

It's important that you know and understand what motivate and drives you so you can take the right affirmative actions to become more confident individual.

Maslow's Hierarchy of Needs

Maslow stated that people are motivated to achieve certain needs and that some needs take precedence over others. Our most basic need is for survival, and this will be the first thing that motivates our behavior. Once that level is fulfilled the next level up is what motivates us, and so on.

1. **Physiological needs** - these are biological requirements for human survival, e.g. air, food, drink, shelter, clothing, warmth, sex, sleep. If these needs are not satisfied the human body cannot function optimally. Maslow considered physiological needs the most important as all the other needs become secondary until these needs are met.

2. **Safety needs** - protection from elements, security, order, law, stability, freedom from fear.

3. **Love and belongingness needs** - after physiological and safety needs have been fulfilled, the third level of human needs is social and involves feelings of belongingness. The need for interpersonal relationships motivates behavior.

Examples include friendship, intimacy, trust, and acceptance, receiving and giving affection and love. Affiliating, being part of a group (family, friends, work).

4. **Esteem needs** - Classified into two categories: (i) esteem for oneself (dignity, achievement, mastery, independence) and (ii) the desire for reputation or respect from others (e.g., status, prestige). Maslow indicated that the need for respect or reputation is most important for children and adolescents and precedes real self-esteem or dignity.

5. **Self-actualization needs** - realizing personal potential, self-fulfillment, seeking personal growth and peak experiences. A desire "to become everything one is capable of becoming" (Maslow, 1987, p. 64).

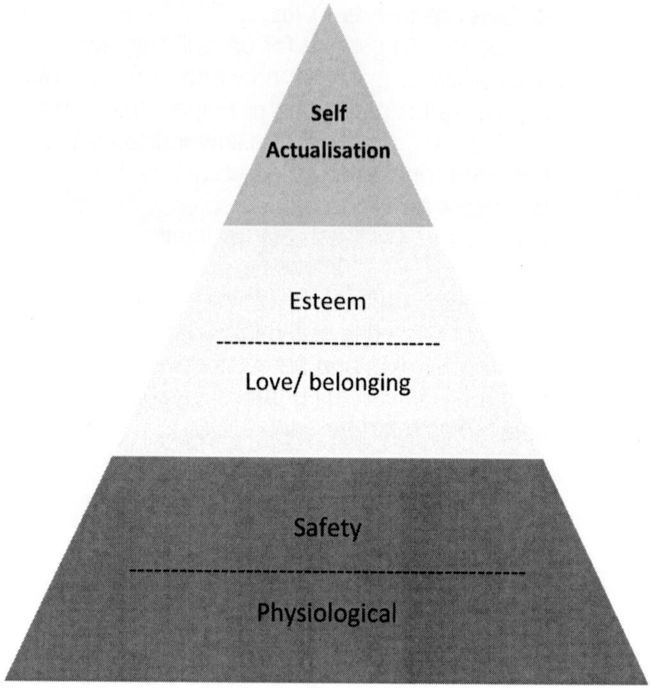

Examples of Determined Individuals

Steve Jobs

Steve was a college dropout however this didn't stop him from dreaming big as he became the founder of Apple. At a young age of 19, Steve Jobs, together with his friend Dan Kottke decided to drop out of College and moved to India instead to find Philosophical Enlightenment. Steve was a determined visionary however at the age of 30, his own company (Apple Inc.) decided to fire him. Can you imagine the company you put your heart and soul into, turning his back against you, leaving you humiliated, depressed, and unemployed? Well, Steve Jobs was determined to overcome that, and he succeeded. A decade after Apple had made him redundant, the company was on the verge of bankruptcy. A time when Microsoft was growing fast and Apple the company was desperate and went back to Steve Jobs. Steve accepted this offer and made Apple one of the most leading and cutting-edge companies on the planet.

Walt Disney

Walt Disney, which is now a household name experienced numerous failures, but he didn't give up. He lost his job as a newspaper editor before; and according to his boss, he lacked imagination and his ideas are no good. He tried to start his own a business but faced bankruptcy. He was literally broke, but his persistence and determination kept him going to try new ideas until he reached success; and once it did, it was overwhelming. He managed to win 22 Academy Awards and established the first Disneyland in California around 1955. Today, the Walt Disney Company brings in billions of dollars annually from movies, theme parks, and merchandise around the world.

A Mother

I once read about a mother who had witnessed her young son being run over and the child was trapped under the car wheels. The driver was left unconscious and there was no help in sight. The story goes that the mother without thinking grabs one corner of the car and lifts it up and allowing her child to escape. This is the amazing strength of will power and determination. Normally this 8 stone (50KG) mother would not be strong enough to move such a weight however the situation was such that her child was hurt, and she had to do whatever it took to save him. There is also another story which tells us about a frightened child who is trapped behind a door and is heard screaming to be let out. The mother then literally rips the door off its hinges to rescue the child. In both stories the mother was so determined and emotionally charged that she didn't consider if her muscles were strong enough to lift the car or break the door down. Her confidence and self-belief were at an all-time high and with the surge of adrenaline she overcame what seemed to be the impossible. Luckily, we don't have to face these types of situations on daily basis.

"Strength does not come from physical capacity. It comes from an indomitable will." Mahatma Gandhi

So, what is this strange thing that gives a person the strength of many people? Well quite simply it is **Determination** and **Will Power**. A source of internal strength that we all possess that comes into play when we are so focused on a goal and an outcome so that nothing else matters. Some would say that it is like the power of a magnifying glass. If a magnifying glass is moved about with no real focus, then a fire will never start however if the power of the sun is harnessed and focused on one point then you get a flame. That flame be the flame of hope and desire that is in all of us. Anyone who has gone through struggles in life must have possessed great determination and will power.

However, will power fades if you are exhausted with what life has thrown at you and nothing seems to go right. I have personally been made redundant 3 times in my career and I had wife and three children to support with mounting debts. I didn't give up but instead was more determined to find a better job. I was successful in finding better jobs and at one time I had to accept a pay cut in order to get back into employment. In the end it worked out well for me and I kept climbing the corporate ladder. Well there is hope for all of us because this will power is not something that is in short supply it can be called upon whenever life is getting on top of you. So just need to dig deep and have faith in yourself. Tell yourself that you have the strength to overcome most if not all of life's challenges.

Tip

Read about others who have overcome major tragedies in their lives and yet they have become true winners and achievers in life.

"It is not where you have come from in life that determines your destiny but the size of your dreams the depth of your conviction and determination and will power you have to achieve them."

When you think about confident and determined people who do you think about?

Is it someone famous or a friend or person at work or in business because all our lives we are surrounded by confident and determined sports men and women such as Roger Federer Rafael Nadal and Novak Djokovic in Tennis or the William sisters.

There are the runners such Usain Bolt the fastest man on the planet at 100 meters.

In Golf There is Tiger Woods, Arnold Palmer, Michelle Wie, Jack Nicklaus, Lexi Thompson, Gary Player, Tom Watson.
In Boxing Muhammad Ali. Katie Taylor, Mary Kom, Floyd Mayweather, Manny Pacquiao, Mike Tyson
In football we have the legends of Pele, Maradona, Cristiano Ronaldo, Sam Kerr, David Beckham, Lucy Bronze, Franz Beckenbauer,
Business: The late Steve Jobs, Bill Gates, Elon Musk, Sir Richard Branson

Altruistic: Mother Theresa, Martin Luther King, Nelson Mandela, Mahatma Gandhi

Pop Idols: Beyonce', Lady Gaga, Rhianna, Adele Freddie Mercury, Elvis Presley, Prince, David Bowie

TV personalities: Oprah Winfrey, Simon Cowell,

Leaders: Winston Church Hill, Indira Gandhi, F.D Roosevelt. Barack Obama, Margaret Thatcher, Abraham Lincoln, Mikhail Gorbachev

All these famous people do or have expressed confidence in their own field yet if we took them outside their comfort zones and they had to lead your life for a day then they too might lack confidence in trying to carry out activities that you normally carry out on a day to day basis. Well you don't have to be famous and rich to be determined and empowered however we all know that these individuals are some examples of how people can stand out. Find your own inspirational heroes if the above listed individuals don't inspire you to be more determined.

What about the rest of us who are not famous and struggling with work or business and trying to make ends meet? We may even feel helpless frustrated and sorry for ourselves, well this is OK for short while. The problems and challenges in life happen to us all the time so accepting the situation is half the battle and then trying to learn something from it is the secret. You have the power to make a difference in your own life and those around you by tapping into this knowledge to learn from our challenges. However, all things happen for a reason, but that reason may not be clear to you at first.

We all know of people out there that want to intimidate us give us orders and tell us what to do, when to do, it and how to do it. These people try and make you feel powerless and insignificant. Many of us tend to do things in life that pleases others with no concern for one's own needs. This is fine if they are trying to help us better our lives and make us stronger and better about our self.

Inspirational Movies with determined individuals

Shawshank Redemption

One of my favorite movies is Shawshank Redemption a prison drama starring Tim Robbins who played Andy Dufresne and Morgan Freeman who played Eliss Boyd Redding 'Red'. Andy is a banker who is put in prison for the murder of his wife and her lover. He pleads innocent but is still imprisoned for life. This banker had hope, that one he would one day get out of jail. He was confident about his knowledge of banking and finance. This empowered him to do things out of the ordinary and get his own way. This knowledge got him out of many troubles and gained benefits such as books for the prison library, trust with the guards and warden. If you haven't seen the film yet, then make sure you do.

The Kings Speech

The other movie that I would recommend is "The Kings Speech" staring Oscar winner Colin Firth, Geoffrey Rush and Helen Bonham Carter. It is a true story of a king's efforts to overcome stammering in order to face his public. Albert played by Colin Firth turn for help to an Australian actor Lionel Logue (Geoffrey Rush) who is working as a speech therapist. It is wonderful psychological journey and discovery about Albert's past. I do not want to spoil the full plot to the film, but it is a triumph over adversity and a fascinating look at relationships between the different classes.

Confidence

Another worthy movie is "Confidence" which was made in 2003 starring Edward Burns, Dustin Hoffman, Andy Garcia and Rachel Weisz. Even though this is crime drama it's worth viewing. Learn from the positive aspects of confidence it rather than the negative aspects of criminality.

Sometimes confident people are not always trusted since there are several confidence tricksters out there that uses their level of confidence to mislead others and influence them to do things that they wouldn't normally do. This is not the courage and confidence that I am talking about but more to do with the courage and confidence that is going to better people's lives. Find a movie or book that will give you fuel for increasing your confidence and self-belief.

Zig Ziggler

A great quote from Zig Ziggler a motivational speaker from the US that I heard many years ago has been inspirational and shows true grit and determination.

"It is not the critic who counts; not the man who points out how the strong man stumbles, or where the doer of deeds could have done them better. The credit belongs to the man who is actually, in the arena, whose face is marred by dust and sweat and blood, who strives valiantly, who errs and comes short again and again, because there is not effort without error and shortcomings; but who does actually strive to do the deed; who knows the great enthusiasm, the great devotion, who spends himself in a worthy cause, who at the best knows in the end the triumph of high achievement and who at the worst, if he fails, at least he fails while daring greatly. So that his place shall never be with those cold and timid souls who know neither victory nor defeat**." Zig Ziglar**

Dr Victor Frankl

Dr. Victor Frankl wrote a book about his experiences as a psychiatrist who barely survived the World War II concentration camps. The book is called: "Man's search for meaning."

He tried to understand what was it that caused some men to suffer and survive through unspeakable horrors while other men gave up and often tried to kill themselves to end their suffering. He concluded that the difference was whether they had a reason (Why) to survive. For example, those that believed they had family waiting for them somewhere showed superhuman determination to survive while many who had no family left, did not.

There must be an emotional "WHY" that fuels the action.

AWAKEN THE GIANT WITHIN, Anthony Robbins

Are you in charge of your life? Or are you being swept away by things that are seemingly out of your control? In AWAKEN THE GIANT WITHIN, Anthony Robbins, the bestselling author of UNLIMITED POWER, shows the reader how to take immediate control of their mental, emotional, physical and financial destiny.

Well it's up to you to become more determined so you too can feel more in control and determined by taking more time for yourself and trying some of the ideas that follow are put forward in this book.

The determination to become more confident is a price worth paying if it's what you really want to achieve

Chapter 7

CONFIDENCE: E for **ESTEEM**

Self Esteem "To wish you were someone else, is to waste the person you are."
Author unknown

As the definition suggests, Self-esteem can often be compared to self-respect, self-worth and self-belief. The true consistent element is the word self. Not surprising this word refers to what you think about yourself. The way you think is based, amongst other things, on your personal feelings, perceptions and belief in yourself. In turn, your level of self-esteem has a direct impact on your behaviuor, not only what you choose to do, but how you react in specific situations.

Life's challenges in general impact on your self-esteem, often fueled by elements beyond your control such as peaks and troughs of daily emotions.

"You yourself, as much as anybody in the entire universe deserve your love and affection." Buddha

Dorothy Wizard of Oz

The wonderful film regularly shown each Christmas time in the western world is the 'Wizard of Oz' written by L Frank Baun and originally published in 1900 however the film was in released in 1939. It's is one of the best-known films' in American popular culture. As many of you may know this is a story about little girl Dorothy Gale who lived on a Kansas farm in Northern America. A neighbor tries to put the dog Toto to sleep so they decide to run away. Dorothy and her dog Toto are blown away in a tornado and land in a fairyland named Oz. On her journey to get home she meets some wonderful characters the Scarecrow, a Tin wood cutter, and the Cowardly Lion. They decide to team up and walk together on the famous yellow brick road to see the Wizard of Oz at Emerald City. Each of the characters was seeking what they want most in life. The Tin man wanted a heart; the Lion to be brave the scarecrow a brain. Each character had to face their fears and overcome a few scary challenges along their way. They arrive at the Emerald City only to be told by the Wizard that they first must kill the Wicked Witch of the West before he will grant their wishes.

They eventually overcome several dangerous challenges and accidentally killed a witch on their journey. Dorothy was now in trouble with the Wicked Witch of the West, who seeks revenge for the death of her sister. She's helped by the Good Witch of the North; Dorothy and her friends return only to find that the Wizard is not real but quite mean and miserable a bit like Ebenezer scrooge character. The wizard craftily addresses everyone's wish but Dorothy's, which is to return home to Kansas. So, once more Dorothy and her friends set out, this time to find the Good Witch of the South. These last adventures end happily with Dorothy and Toto returning home, thanks to something she had with her all along the ruby slippers and to truly wish and believe in getting back to her home.

This same thing that Dorothy came to discover can also help you as how you look at yourself effects how you feel. Not only that, if you think negatively about yourself, you're less likely to participate in social events etc. The power to change and become more confident is in the palm of your hands if you believe more in your own abilities.

Tackling Low Self Esteem:

So how do you tackle low self-esteem?

(If you have been clinically diagnosed as depressed then please seek further professional medical advice)

Unfortunately, there isn't a simple answer, but the only certainty is that no matter how many people say wonderful positive things about you, unless you believe it, your self-esteem will not improve. For you to increase your self-esteem, you must choose to change the way you look at yourself and feel and its only **YOU** can make these choices. Take time to relax rest and make time for yourself. Only when you are calm can you begin to look at your situation objectively without too much negative emotions getting in your way. Whenever you are in a highly emotional state your perception can become distorted or disproportionate (we call this emotional **hijacking'**) only when you are calm can a healthy self-esteem emerge and force off the likely 'hijacking'. Once you have reviewed your situation in a calm manner you can begin to look for the positives. Self-affirming words and phrases will mean more to you if you believe in them and steadily, they do begin to challenge your present way of thinking and force you to look at the positive in your life. Rather than waiting for others to tell you nice things, remind yourself of them every day.

"I CAN is 100 times more important than IQ." Caroline Coyle

Explore and engage in activities that you enjoy and ones that you can lose yourself in, help to deflect your attention away from the negatives and challenges you are facing at present. This will help bring a healthier balance in your life. If you spend too much time on your own, you will begin to fall back into your old ways, but equally if you spend too much time with others who are not supportive will you begin to compare yourself with their situation and rate yourself against them. Keeping a healthy balance in life between yourself and others is vital to a balanced level of self-esteem.

Recognizing self esteem

The following list will help you recognize low self-esteem. Once you understand the triggers and source of low self-esteem, the easier it is to tackle it.

1. Social withdrawal and less social conformity

2. Anxiety and emotional turmoil

3. Lack of social skills and self-confidence. Depression and/or bouts of sadness

5. Self-neglect Eating disorders

6. Inability to see yourself squarely – to be fair to yourself

7. Accentuate the negative

8. Exaggerated concern over what you imagine other people think

9. Worrying whether you have treated others badly

10. Reluctance to take on challenges trust your own opinion

Let's look at some of this definition of confidence in more detail.

Confidence is defined as a feeling which emanates from a belief. The stronger the belief you have the stronger the feeling. The more and more you believe in something the greater faith you will have. You will have a greater certainty about yourself and the situations you face once you are able to appreciate some of the wonderful qualities that you possess. You will become self-assured that you too can be confident.

The Webster's definition states

The State of Mind characterized by one's Reliance on oneself, or Circumstances; a Feeling of Self-sufficiency; such Assurance as leads to a feeling of Security; Self-reliance; - often with self-prefixed. Having self-reliance being bold undaunted as confident as the falcon's flight.

Just imagine if the falcon had doubt in its ability to fly then it would never take off and yet at one point in their lives young falcon chicks could not fly. However, their parents coaxed them out of the nest and when they are ready, they are pushed out when their feathers have grown. This means that there is no room for mistakes and the new fledgling falcon has no choice but to flap its wings. After a short while it gains enough confidence and it soars through the sky seeks the freedom of the sky while a cool breeze pass over its wings. This falcon then starts to master the art of flight. We don't normally look up in the sky and say to ourselves that bird looks like it is having trouble flying today maybe it is lacking in confidence that is unless of course it is injured and then it has to learn to fly again. Animals and birds have an innate ability to do certain things like fly, run, jump and swim. Human beings have the same abilities but not to the same extent and they tend to take longer to learn these physical skills.

When you see a baby who is learning to crawl or walk suddenly falls over you don't say well back in your push chair for you, it looks like your walking days are over and I will have to push you for the rest of your life. Of course, not that would be absurd. The baby and the parent would keep wanting to try harder so that the new toddler if physically able to could learn to walk with confidence and yes there will be more falls and bruises along the way but that is just a small price to pay to be able to walk. A supportive parent would always hug the child and praise them as a reward for being able to walk and taking those first few steps. Now you would not do that for every new step they took until they are an adult then that would be silly. However, we would reward and compliment that child in different ways as they grow up to adult hood.

Why have I used this simple analogy of learning to walk it's because sometimes in life we try something new that often we are not that good at first. We may even have started a new hobby like golf or have been asked to speak in public for the first time. You may get stressed and upset that things did not go well with this new hobby or speech, so we associate bad uncomfortable feelings about this new experience. You may have chosen to quit and no longer want to face those uncomfortable feelings and yet that is the price that needs to be paid in order to become better at something. Every new experience in life has in it a price tag in order be good at it and a steep learning curve. When I first began to learn a second martial art such as aikido after training in Ju Jitsu for nearly 30 years, I found that was not as easy as I thought. I had to retrain my body and mind to move in a slightly different way and emphasis on internal structure and core movement. What worked in Ju Jitsu didn't always work in aikido and vice versa. I began to doubt my own ability and it had a knock on my self-esteem, but I was keen to learn and improve and over time I became a black belt in this martial art as well but didn't give up but kept going. I had to relearn like a beginner and take on a steep learning curve and be prepared for criticism and support. If you are prepared to take the knocks and pick your self-back up with more vigor and determination, then you will be rewarded with greater abilities and skills and an enormous boost to your confidence.

"All you need in this life is ignorance and confidence; then success is sure." Mark Twain Letter to Mrs. Foote, Dec. 2, 1887 US humorist, novelist, short story author, & wit (1835 - 1910)

"Believe in yourself!

Have faith in your abilities! Without a humble but reasonable confidence in your own powers you cannot be successful or happy." Norman Vincent Peale (1898 - 1993)

Masks we wear

Have you ever put on an act for someone to make you appear a certain way? Maybe you want to make people think that you know it all, or that you don't need any one or that you are a very busy person? Or perhaps there is something about you that you are uncomfortable with and rather than being exposed you cover it up by putting on a 'happy' face. These are some of the masks we wear to make us appear a certain way.

Masks are a part of daily life; everyone wears different masks for different situations. For example:

- When you go to work what type of person do you become?
- When you are with friends, who are you then?
- When you are with your family who are you?
- Who are you when you first wake in the morning?

Why do we wear masks?

The main reason for wearing a mask is self-protection. Whenever, we express our self, i.e. when we show some type of emotion e.g. joy, sadness, love, hate, satisfaction, frustration, courage, fear, hope and despair, we are showing our true self which is vulnerable to the outside world. We fear rejection, ridicule, and basically any response that devalues us.

What do we do about these masks?

The obvious answer is to take these masks off and be who you really are. But this is not as easy as it seems. A better solution is to take small steps to make the changes.

You may be a coping with a new relationship a new job or with meeting new people in general. To the world you show that everything is fine and it's all great and that you enjoy meeting new people. However, inside, you may be in a state of discomfort, learning as quickly as you can at being someone else rather than being you. Sometimes adjusting to the fact that you must adapt to new situations and relationships and finding it hard to deal with change. It is natural to feel uncomfortable in new situations however if you allow others to know your true self and you let your guard down to those you trust as it will be a wise move. People who can be themselves and let their mask down in the right situations are a lot more relaxed and happier with their lives. I do realize that you may have a few bad experiences when you let you guard down, and you were hurt as a result. However, do not let these experiences dictate your chance of a better more confident you.

After all you are only human like the rest of us! Find someone you trust to confide in and tell them how you really feel. You will be amazed to find that we all wear mask in some form or other. 'A problem shared is a problem halved' is the famous saying so do share with someone close and understanding.

"It takes courage to grow up and become who you really are." - E.E Cummings

"Let the world know you as you are, not as you think you should be, because sooner or later, if you are posing, you will forget the pose, and then where are you?" - Fanny Brice.

MY MASK

The mask I wear is the mask you see but is not the real me

The mask I show to the world is my alter ego and I hide the person inside

Each day I wear a mask I lose my-self

Each day I want to be brave enough to show my true self

Each day Only to those that know me well do I be true to my-self and you

One day my confidence will be strong enough to reveal the inner me and that day is today.

Motivation

Definition:

Enthusiasm for doing something/the need or reason for doing something, motivation derives its name from the Latin word **movere** to move or act.

You may be motivated by pain or pleasure. People either take action to avoid painful experiences or take action to gain pleasurable ones. For example, at work you may be motivated by promise of pay rise or bonus so you work longer hours because you are thinking about the holiday you can take or the new car and clothes that you might buy with the extra money. You may be motivated by the threat of being fired and made redundant if you don't perform better. You are then thinking of the pain of being in debt and not being able to pay the bills.

This is a simple carrot and stick look at motivation. However, you and I are more complex humans then this we have our own goals and values and beliefs that must be met for us to act. We also have internal (Intrinsic) and external (extrinsic) motivation.

You might know how to motivate yourself but how do you motivate others and create the right environment. It is always best to get to know the people in your team and assess what type of things motivates them.

- Is it money?
- Is the recognition that they are doing a good job?
- Do they have the right mix of tasks that motivates them?
- Do members of your staff gain good feelings once they have achieved their task?
- Are they given enough opportunities for their voice to be heard and so contributing to ideas?

Revisiting Abraham Maslow's needs hierarchy model encompass several needs that are important for motivation.

1) Physiological needs safety needs, desire for food, water air and shelter

2) Need for a safe and stable environment and free from pain or discomfort

3) Social need for affiliation or belonging such as companionship or love.

4) Need or desire for achievement, self-worth and recognition and attention.

5) Esteem needs accomplishment, self-respect to achieve level of importance

6) Need to know or understand

7) Aesthetic needs

8) Self-actualization truth, meaning justice, wisdom

9) Transcendence

People don't normally move through the levels of need unless these needs are met along the way. Other needs that are also important are the need to reproduce and pass on our genes by becoming a parent.

Ask yourself are these above nine needs currently being met for you?

If not, which areas require your attention more so then others.

If a number of these needs are not met, then your self-belief may be low and so bring about low self-esteem and confidence. If we do not know how to motivate ourselves in the right way, then it is unlikely that we are going to act. We all need a goal and a direction in life to aim at. It underpins almost everything we do and without it we don't have direction, purpose, passion, ideas or dreams.

We require something that we can believe in and have the passion and conviction to pursue.

How motivated are you?

Let me tell give you a small test of your motivation level.

Would you walk across a steel bridge 12 inches wide by 50 feet long, if it was only 1 foot off the ground?

Most people would say yes.

What if this bridge was 10 feet off the ground? Some would do it to challenge themselves and others of you would need a good reason to do it. Some maybe scared of heights.

What if I offered you £100 or $100 would you walk across? Yes, or No

What amount of money would motivate you to take a risk like this? $1000, $50,000

What if the bridge was across two tall buildings that are 1000 feet high?

What would motivate you to walk across this bridge to the other side and without a harness?

Some of you will have already decided that you would never do it and others have a price in mind to make the perilous walk. Is it worth risking your life for the money?

Now take the same situation but this time there is a there is 100 km per hour winds blowing and ice is forming on the bridge. Now would you walk across for the same amount of money or would you say no way you have to be crazy to walk across.

LITTLE POCKET OF CONFIDENCE

Let me change a few things to this daring scenario. This time I play the part of an evil villain and I am standing at the other side of the bridge and holding the person you love the most over the edge and threaten to throw them off if you didn't make the long walk across to save them. (The loved one maybe your child, wife, husband, best friend, partner)

Well you know the answer. Without hesitation you would do whatever it took to save your loved one or find someone very quickly who would. Your motivation is at an all-time high and your confidence level is given little thought. Yes, you would be scared but the reasons are so strong that you are prepared to take all the risks for no pay and the reward would be the saving a loved one's life. We know that soldiers in war zones and members of the public have put themselves in harm's way in order to save others, people's lives and an act of self-sacrifice.

We would not normally have to face this level of danger and make these difficult choices however we know that your motivation will sometimes take a set back and it can trigger a chain reaction of negative feelings. However, the more we understand why that happens the better equipped you'll be to handle it should it ever happen again. It is important to keep nourishing your confidence by understanding what type of needs require fulfilling in order to keep you motivated and so raise your confidence.

The key thing to remember is that the most powerful of all motivation is that which you have created from within" Intrinsic motivation" rather than extrinsic. You can have better control of what happens inside your head then the external situations that face you.

By making your intrinsic motivation high then it is like the analogy of a large oak tree and its roots are many and deep into the ground to hold it firm and keep it strong. What I mean by this is that a majestic strong oak tree will remain upright and survive the most violent of storm conditions provided the roots are deep. This is also the same for our confidence levels. Our internal motivation needs to be high in order to tackle the next challenge in your life. It might be that you must speak in public, but you are scared. By working on those empowering beliefs and visualize doing well in your speech as well as the benefit to the audience then you will become more confident as a result.

In such a situation where you have a conflict, you need to take a step back and look at your situation. It's now not a matter of whether you're motivated or not, it's now a matter of what you deem to be important, not just now but in the future. Once you've taken that fresh look and sorted out what's important, you will in turn reinstate your internal motivation to make it happen but only if you believe it to be important.

If you have some small doubts about what you are doing and somewhat nervous then you may find it helpful to anchor your thoughts to something tangible. For example, what things can you use to remind you that you that the reason that you are doing this for. What will trigger positive emotions? It may be a song, famous quote, picture, item of clothing... Whatever it is, you might want to keep them at hand to give you a constant reminder as why you can be more confident. Motivation is simply a state of mind, but it only comes from what you truly believe and desire. It can't be faked or created; you must want something to be motivated to achieve it. The stronger your belief the stronger your motivation and in turn the stronger your emotions, mental/physical health and general state of mind. Remember, that as with empowerment, it's only down to you and the choices you make.

Ability is what you're capable of doing. Motivation determines what you do. Attitude determines how well you do it." - Lou Holtz

The following extract illustrates how easy it is to change your mindset and in turn, revitalize your motivation.

If I feel depressed, I will sing.

If I feel sad I will laugh.

If I feel ill I will double my labor.

If I feel fear, I will plunge ahead.

If I feel inferior, I will wear new garments.

If I feel uncertain I will raise my voice.

If I feel poverty, I will think of wealth to come.

If I feel incompetent, I will think of past success.

If I feel insignificant, I will remember my goals.

Today I will be the master of my emotions.

Og Mandino, "The Greatest Salesman in the World"

The best fuel for your motivation is often a good story and what a better one than your own. By keeping a daily diary of how your feeling and what things you've encountered will help you to take a step back and look at your life decisively. It will also begin to record the steps your taking and what better motivation do you need than our own success. Remember "Today I will be the master of my emotions!"

Esteem in more detail:

Esteem Definition:

Definition: a favorable appraisal of a person who possesses qualities estimated as of significant value. A feeling of being honored and self-respected.

There are two versions of esteem needs -

1. The need for the respect of and recognition by others, and

2. The need for self-respect.

Respect: Respecting yourself and others

Definition of respect:

Treating someone with consideration avoiding the 'I's - interfering, interrupting, insulting, and injuring not offending, corrupting or tempting.

You've probably heard the phrase – treat others how you want to be treated but have you ever stopped to wonder what this really means?

If you know people out there who never gives anyone else's feelings a second thought; would prefer looking cool in front of friends rather than losing face. Has disregard to teachers or those in authority, parents or treat the police as stupid or inferior then these individuals have a respect problem.

Respecting yourself

If you don't respect yourself, no one else will. It's as simple as that.

Examples of not respecting your self

- Not eating healthily is disrespecting your body as is smoking, taking drugs and not exercising.

- Spending too much time on social media or watching television, not reading or learning new things is disrespecting your mind

- Throwing your personal items around, keeping an untidy room or losing things all the time mean you are disrespecting your possessions.

If you think you have an issue with self-respect think about setting some rules for yourself which will guide you and consider some helpful affirmations.

Suggested affirmations:

- I take care of my things - my clothes, mobile phone, gifts from others, etc.

- I care about my body and eat at least five pieces of fruit and vegetables a day

- I walk for 15 to 30 minutes every day

- I do things that are positive and makes me feel comfortable

- I stand up for myself and my views

- I ask for help when I need it

It's important that you learn to respect yourself when it comes to looking after your body and mind. In the long term your new self-respect will allow others to model your positive behavior for example children will learn from their parents, guardians, peers and friends. If you are not taking care of yourself and your things, those are the habits they will learn.

Respecting others

You might have heard of several governments 'respect agenda'. It's about tackling the growing levels of anti-social behavior we have on the streets, in schools and elsewhere. You may have been a victim of it yourself. I suspect what this agenda is trying to do is remind people that if we all want to live together in a peaceful way, we need to have respect for others around us.

Respecting others is about keeping a check on your behavior and attitude when it comes to dealing and communicating with others and respecting their possessions. It's not about being weak or caving in. It's about considering their feelings or opinions and not making them feel small or insignificant and it's also recognizing that they have rights too.

Examples of disrespecting others include:

- Interrupting them when they are speaking
- Acting like their opinion doesn't matter
- Not listening to people who might be trying to help (e.g. doctors, nurses, teachers)
- Not looking after something you've borrowed from a friend
- Using bad language
- Gossiping about people behind their backs
- Hurting someone or damaging their possessions
- Being late when you are meeting someone

If you recognize yourself in any of the above examples start changing your behavior or avoid individuals that act this way.

Set some rules up for yourself and keep to them. See examples below a set of rules and affirmations.

Additional Possible affirmations:

- I consider the feelings of others before I impart my own opinion
- I keep calm with my family or friends
- I listen to professionals giving me advice, especially those trying to help me
- If I say I'm going to do something, I do it. If I can't I let the person know.

Reacting under pressure

Being under pressure and stressed out physically and mentally can be very tough and there are lots of people out there that can give you advice. You may get sick of hearing what you 'should' do or 'what's best for you and sometimes it can sound like everyone is telling you what to do. Instead of getting angry and telling them where to go with their 'advice' consider taking a more respectful route.

For example, people may tell you what to do to find a new job instead of ignoring advice why not pause to think or do your own research on the internet to see if they are right. Also ask any experts you know and get the facts. If you disagree with the person respect them enough just to say 'thank you very much, I'll look into it' instead of losing your cool and disrespecting them.

Remember that if you want others to treat you with respect, you must give them the respect they deserve. Think about your own behavior towards yourself and if you are not happy, put some rules in place to change things. Respect yourself enough to do it – and stick to it!

Gratitude

"Gratitude is not only the greatest of virtues, but the parent of all others." - Cicero

"To educate yourself for the feeling of gratitude means to take nothing for granted, but to always seek out and value the kind that will stand behind the action. Nothing that is done for you is a matter of course. Everything originates in a will for

the good, which is directed at you. Train yourself never to put off the word or action for the expression of gratitude."- Albert Schweitzer

Showing a sense of gratitude does not necessarily have to relate to something tangible, in fact, what you will most likely find after reading this section is that you feel gratitude for things that you can't necessarily see. Finding people and things to be thankful for can sometimes seem difficult especially if your life is in constant turmoil. For you to feel gratitude you must first appreciate what someone has done for you. Often, we expect so much of others that we forget that, a lot of the time, others who help us out are doing so because they want to, not because they must. The tendency however is to expect the things in life that we shouldn't necessarily expect to happen. For example, most people wouldn't think to show gratitude to their local water company for providing, clean running water to your home, their local fire or police service. However, if you were to live in parts of Africa where such a commodity is extremely rare, then should you suddenly begin to show gratitude if you were not able to get access to clean water for a few days or week.

Ultimately, we all do things for others because often, we want to. Ask yourself, how many times have you said thank you or shown your appreciation to those people who have gone out of their way to support you? It's easy to answer the question with a sharp yes.

How many times you have shown your gratitude, not felt it or shown it! We can do things because we liked to be loved and feel wanted. It's one of the most fundamental motivators in life and the reason why we do so many things, though a lot of us may not admit it. When you go out of your way to help someone, support them, a show of gratitude in return is sometimes enough reward to encourage the same behavior again and again.

If you are a parent, brother or sister to someone a friend to others a grandparent, uncle or aunty, foster parents, then there will be plenty of people to be show gratitude to. If you are a parent, then the ability to demonstrate gratitude towards your child is paramount to their development. Through childhood and into later teenage years, children thrive on feeling wanted, appreciated and loved. Being loved and wanted is a fundamental motivator in life and as parent, your demonstration of gratitude will encourage positive behaviors in your child. So, remember, no matter how small and relatively insignificant the gesture, show your gratitude and say thank you or reward your child. From the impromptus hug, to a painting they give you because they think you want it, say thank you and reciprocate their gesture to encourage further positive behavior.

Act and show gratitude

List 3 people you feel that you can show gratitude for and tell them how much you care and love them.

You can

- Speak to them face to face
- Write them a letter
- Send them an e-mail
- Buy them a present
- Cook them a meal

- Take them out for a meal
- Give them a hug whatever makes you and them feel better. If you are religious or spiritual, then show your gratitude and appreciation to your maker or the universe for all the great things in life such as:
- Love
- Passion
- Free will
- A child's smile, flowers,
- Friendship tears and laughter
- A wonderful sunset or sunrise
- Butterflies
- Birds
- Your pet dog or cat or
- Whatever sparks your emotions

Chapter 8

CONFIDENCE N for **NECESSITY**

You may have come across this quote "Necessity is the mother of invention "by Plato the Greek philosopher

What this means is the when something in your life has become so important and necessary then you invent and create ideas to solve the situation at hand. If you are cold, then you seek warmth or light a fire. If you are hungry you look for food in the fridge or in the wild forage for something to eat or kill if you are a meat eater as its essential in your life in order to survive.

Ask yourself a question.

How important is it for you to be more confident and to change your habits?

Is it something that is an absolute necessity that is going to make a real difference to your life or is it just a wish and a want which you can live without?

For many of us what we need in life is more important than what we may want. Let me explain.

Some people want to something in life such as a bigger and faster car, to lose weight, make more money, have a bigger house. These types of things can be achieved with work and effort and at the same time you could live and survive without them. So, this means that these are not necessary for your daily survival.

However, things like clean drinking water, air, food, warmth, are necessary to survive. To some people exercise and to do adrenaline driven activities is necessary to feel alive. These could be thrill seeking adrenaline junkies and that need to jump out of planes, walk on fire, bungee jump, swim with sharks to feel alive. While others are happy to go for a walk in the park or sit down in front of the television or in front of their mobile phones.

How important out of a score of 10 is having more confidence to you?

If it's a 3 out of 10 then it's not that important to you and you are unlikely to take action to achieve more confidence. If it's a 6 or 7 then you may start to take some action, make some progress then if a difficult challenge comes along then this may hold you back from achieving your goal.

If you are an 8 or 9 what will it take to make you a 10.

If you are a genuine 10 then you will make a change to your habits and take the **necessary** steps to be more confident.

If you want to be better at relationships, then it's **necessary** to change

If you keep on being rejected when applying for new jobs, then it's **necessary** to change.

If your doctor tells you that if you don't stop drinking as you have a medical condition that will kill you then it's **necessary,** change your habits

If you are hungry and have not eaten or drunk liquids for days or weeks, then it's **necessary** to eat in order to survive

Belief in a creator, God is **necessary** for some people.

For some people having companionship and relationships is **necessary** in order to live a life worthwhile while others can survive without contact with others for years.

For some people having 8-10 hours' sleep a day is necessary while others 4-6 hours is enough.

If you are stranded on a dessert island you become very inventive or you die very quickly.

Once you have a real necessity to be more confidence then this becomes a score of 10 out of 10 then you will be inventing ways to means to help you become more confident.

iPhone story

On 29th June 2007 the first iPhone was released.

The business world was wondering if people were prepared to pay large sums of money for this new and expensive technology as many people had blackberries for their work phones. The company that made Blackberry phones didn't think there was a place for personal phones like iPhones as mobile phones were then really for business and no one would pay so much for an iPhone. Steve Jobs the founder of Apple computers created such an incredible need, necessity and hype for the iPhone that it was a must have item and so much so that people queued for days to purchase one. Many people who had a Blackberry for work however they also had an iPhone for personal use. Over a short few years many businesses moved from Blackberry. Motorola and Nokia to iPhones and the rest was history. This later evolved to iPad and apple mac purchases. The Android phones and companies like Samsung have now also taken a good share of the market because of their advances in technology.

The need and necessity drove the mobile phone market. What is the need and necessity that's going to drive your behavior and internal market of your brain? Build the necessary skills and habits to make you increase your confidence

Let's explore some of the benefits of having more confidence

Let's consider some of the benefits of having more confidence

- Ability to make more friends
- Ability to speak in public
- Have more success at interviews and gain better jobs
- Overcome fear and anxiety
- Have more energy
- Have a greater chance of success in business?
- Become more employable

- Can make you more attractive to others
- Greater happiness
- Less self-doubt
- Better health and well being

There are plenty of more benefits I could list however these are enough for you to think about.

Are you making the necessary steps to becoming more confident?

If the reason for you to become more confident is because you want to perform better at interviews to secure a better job and prospects, then plan.

The following steps below now are **necessary** for you to be more confident. If you don't take the actions below then your desire and need is not important enough for you.

- Learn and read books about how to improve at interview techniques

- Practice answering questions with a friend
- Record your self be your own best coach
- Ask for feedback from the person who interviewed of how you can improve
- Learn how to have better body language

If the reason you want to be more confident is because you want to speak in public, then the following steps below are **necessary** to become more confident.

- Seek out and create opportunities at work or your personal life where you can speak up and be heard
- Listen to motivational videos on TED talks on YouTube
- Read books about overcoming fear and anxiety
- Learn how to relax in breath better when in having to speak in public

- Prepare notes that will keep you on track
- Be passionate about you message

Keep in Simple Silly/ Stupid an easy way to remember is K.I.S.S

- Tell the audience what you are going to tell them then
- Tell them and then summarize and
- Tell them what you have just told them about

Make your reasons so big for wanting to have more confidence that it will drive you to do and take actions. It then becomes necessary for you to do the things you need to do to succeed.

If you are gasping for air under water because you have been trapped under a boat, then you will do whatever steps necessary to survive.

LITTLE POCKET OF CONFIDENCE

Find the reason why you need to become more confident and build a plan to achieve it and make it an absolute necessity to succeed.

Chapter 9

CONFIDENCE: C for **COMMUNICATION**

"The single biggest problem in communication is the illusion that it has taken place." – George Bernard Shaw

Albert Mehrabian research on communication would suggest that when we communicate to others there is an importance placed on what form of communication we use. Born in 1939 to an Armenian family living in Iran, is Professor Emeritus of Psychology at the University of California, Los Angeles. Although he originally trained as an engineer

His early research showed how we communicate this can be a combination of the words we use the tone and inflexion as well as body language.

His findings would suggest that the level of importance placed on how we communicate is more with body language.

7% The words we use
38% The Tone of voice and inflection
55% Body language and facial expression.

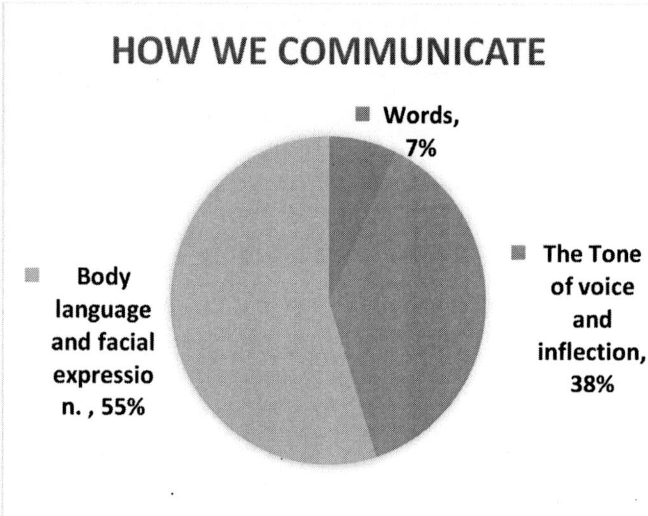

So, when we are presenting or just communicating with others this is worth bearing in mind that body language is one of the most important part of communicating. This may be different for those that spend most of their working life in front or a computer or on the telephone so the written or spoken communication needs to be more focused on. Sometimes we focus too much on what we are going to say rather than the style and delivery. People will make judgements about us on the way we carry ourselves in public as well as the way we talk and dress. It's therefore important that we make a good impression. Since body language is very important part of our communication it would seem only right that we focus on this area to help you with improving your level of confidence and delivery. When it comes to body language, we are very close to the animal kingdom. When we are proud and confident like lions, we stand tall and show others how big and domineering we are. When we are shy and scared, we cower down to others and make ourselves look smaller and less threatening. Human body language is more complex than this since we express many forms of facial expression and hand and body gestures that have many meanings. The core elements in all communications stay the same. Our internal dialogue in our minds can be reflected in our voices and body language we display to others.

Since Mehrabian's early research several other studies have analyzed the relative contributions of verbal and nonverbal signals under more naturalistic situations. Take for example a study in 1970, using video tapes shown to the subjects, analyzed the communication of submissive/dominant attitude and found that all types of non-verbal cues combined, especially body posture could have 4 times the effect of verbal cues. Another study in 1992, dealing with the communication of happy/sad mood, found that hearing words spoken in a "flat" voice was about also 4 times more influential than facial expressions seen in a film with no sound. This shows you that different studies may reach very different conclusions dependent on methodology.

Make our butterflies fly in formation

RAJ SOREN

Sketch by Jyoti Soren

For some people talking in public can be more frightening than thought of death. Our mouths can dry up and our voice chords can feel tight. Our voices may sound squeaky and for some reason we cannot seem to be able to function normally because of our fear has gripped us. Our tongues can seem tied up; we cannot make out a straight sentence we can't remember what we were supposed to talk about. We may start mumbling and fidgeting and dropping our notes, we have little eye contact with the audience. We start to sweat profusely and feel sick or giddy and all we want is the ground to swallow you up so no one can see you suffering and embarrassed.

Well that was me for much of my early life as I found speaking in public very nerve wracking and now, I teach martial arts several times a week and run seminars to groups of up to 500 plus people at a time. I have also spoken and performed on stage in front of 1000s of people. However, my journey to becoming more confident didn't happen overnight, it took many failures and going outside my comfort zones but believing that I could be better. You may not be as nervous as me which is great. If we are truly honest with ourselves then we all have some nerves and butterflies in or stomachs.

"It's OK to have butterflies in your stomach. Just get them to fly in formation."- Dr Rob Gilbert

We just must learn how to **make our butterflies fly in formation**. If you say that you never show signs of nerves and that you are already super confident then how can you relate to others and help them if you have not experienced some of these fears and concerns. I believe having a few nerves and worries are fine and is very natural since it all forms part of our fear or flight response. It shows that we care about what we are about to present on and the impact it is going to have on the audience as well as our selves.

The ability to master this nervous energy is vitally important in order make a change to your level of confidence. Our natural reaction for our bodies is to sense and avoid danger. If we go back to the cave man/woman days, we were hunter gathers living in caves and forest dwellings and they would have faced danger daily. When we search for food and shelter the cave man would come across fierce animals or tribes' men from other parts of the forest. The natural reaction would be to run and hide and seek safety or take up arms to defend their ground possibly to their death. They good news is that we no longer live and caves or run away from prehistoric animals, yet we still experience fight or flight responses.

The LIFE of YOU – show

Let's look at modern world communication and reality television such X-factor to Britain's and Americans got talent and I am celebrity get me out here.

It doesn't matter whether you like these types of programs or not they are still popular. They all have a common theme. The shows have a victim or a hero or heroine who is under the scrutiny of the magnifying glass of mass entertainment and media. If these people can communicate their likeability factor and can show that they are very human, and they make mistakes and just be themselves. This helps them to be relatable and if they have some talent and can illicit emotional reactions, then they have a good chance of winning peoples votes.

You too are in your own show it's called the **Life of you**. Those around you are also commenting on how you talk, walk and the body language you display. The art of communication is fundamental to how you want to portray to others that you are a confident person.

So, what does this all have to do with your situation? Well more than you would first think. Our brains have developed over many millions of years, yet our instinct and fearful feelings are hard wired into our natural body defenses. It's up to us if we can tame and use this natural reaction to help or hinder us. When we are normally less confident about doing something due to a few reasons such as: -

- Lack of knowledge
- Lack of experience to carry out that task
- Fear of what others would think
- Poor self-belief and self-worth
- Negative associations with the task at hand

Once we have identified with this then we know how to best tackle the reason.

How to overcome these nerves and stay focused?

If it is lack of knowledge, then this is area of research that you need investment your time into. Develop a plan of action of getting to know your subject matter. Are you presenting about something at work or for business or even college?

Have you devised a simple method of making notes and referring to them for your presentation?

For many years I have used mind maps since I learnt about them. They were invented by Tony Buzan a world-renowned memory expert as a very effective method of note taking. Once a mind map is drawn and used a few times it no longer needs to be referred to. A mind map is an easy way to brainstorm thoughts organically without worrying about order and structure. It allows you to visually structure your ideas to help with analysis and recall.

A mind map is a diagram for representing tasks, words, concepts, or items linked to and arranged around a central concept or subject using a non-linear graphical layout that allows the user to build an intuitive framework around a central concept. A mind map can turn a long list of monotonous information into a colorful, memorable and highly organized diagram that works in line with your brain's natural way of doing things.

How to draw mind maps?

Find a large sheet of paper ideally a blank sheet.

Mind maps involve drawing pictures and using colors pens to help you bring your thoughts to life.

- Begin with the main concept.

- First determine the main purpose of your mind map and write it down
- Add branches to the main concept. Now that you have determined the main purpose of your mind map, add branches that will outline the most basic subtopics.
- Explore topics by adding more branches.
- Add images and colors.

If you are delivering a presentation what is the title and how can this be represented in diagrammatic form. Make this the center piece of your mind map and make it bold and colorful.

Nelson Mandela

One of the greatest speeches I believe in recent times was by Nelson Mandela's in his inaugural speech in Pretoria on the 11 May 1994. He talks about how great and powerful we can all be.

"Our deepest fear is not that we are inadequate. Our deepest fear is that we are powerful beyond measure. It is our light, not our darkness that most frightens us. We ask ourselves, who am I to be brilliant, gorgeous, talented, fabulous?

Who are you not to be? You are a child of God. You're playing small does not serve the world. There is nothing enlightened about shrinking so that other people won't feel insecure around you. We are all meant to shine, as children do. We were born to make manifest the glory of God that is within us. It's not just in some of us; it's in everyone. And as we let our own light shine, we unconsciously give other people permission to do the same. As we are liberated from our own fear, our presence automatically liberates others."

There are some profound words that speak out to all of us if we are prepared to listen to them and act on them. What this speech tells us is that we are all born with courage and the seed of power and greatness and by shying away from it serves no purpose.

Don't quit! I am reminded of the quote from Vince Lombardi, "Winners never quit, and quitters never win." This is so true! You may have to back up, turn around, or take a completely different approach, but you can never stop trying to get past the present roadblock. Communicate with others with passion and enthusiasm and your confidence will shine through.

"Having a strong desire or being successful does not mean that you are going to feel great all the time. No matter how enlightened I become, I will not be positive all the time. You have to understand the swing of the pendulum. It must swing back and forth. The only other alternative is to sit still in neutral, which is precisely what most people do." - Thomas D. Willhite

Chapter 10

CONFIDENC**E**: E for **ENTHUSIASM**

"I began to realize how important it was to be an enthusiast in life. He taught me that if you are interested in something, no matter what it is, go at it at full speed ahead. Embrace it with both arms, hug it, love it and above all become passionate about it. Lukewarm is no good. Hot is no good either. White hot and passionate is the only thing to be." Roald Dahl, My Uncle Oswald

Enthusiasm has its origins from the Greek word **entheos** which originally meant inspiration or possession by a divine afflatus or by the presence of a god. These days it means intense enjoyment, interest or approval. Enthusiasm requires passion and the love of the activity that you are taking part in. This passion and enthusiasm can be used to enthuse others about ideas, or it can rally people together for good or even bad causes.

Think back when you were at school or college, which lessons did you enjoy the most.

What subject was it? Was its Geography, Science, Mathematics, English, History, Art or was it just the subject where the teacher and lecturer was most enthusiastic.

The enthusiastic teacher may have attracted you to the subject so much so that you wanted to learn more about it and make sure that you made extra special effort to ensure that the homework was completed on time and to a good standard. You would have most likely remembered many facts and figures from those lessons even though it was many years ago. Some of you would have taken up the subject for further study and have become teachers, lecturers and professors. What do you remember about those lessons that were boring and had no life in them? Were you falling asleep in class because the subject was taught in a flat uninteresting manner with no real meaning given to the words and subject? These same teachers must have originally enjoyed the subject that they wanted to teach but lost the love for teaching because of the stress put on these hard-working individuals. Just because an individual can remember facts and figures to pass and exam and to learn to become teacher does not make them a good teacher. It is a teacher's passion and enthusiasm that can affect the lives of students and by the love of their subject and need to share knowledge by storytelling that makes them a good teacher.

Now think about when you talk to others around you or when you are to give presentations at work and in business are the audience going to see an enthusiastic person who truly believes in what they are saying. Or are they going to see a timid individual that doesn't know their subject and who is ill prepared. Others in the room half listening to you may be talking or preoccupied with texting on their phones or typing on they laptops. So how can you make an impact with your message if it is not impacting on yourself?

Just think if you hear a funny story or joke or watch a comedy on the television you begin to laugh so much that others around you also laugh. This laughter then becomes infectious and the whole room starts to laugh with you. If you give someone around you a genuine smile, then they will also return the smile.

"What you give out to the world around you will be reflected back at you."

Rocket science

Imagine a rocket taking off from its launching pad. It burns fuel to produce thrust to lift off the ground and propel itself forward with enough force to escape earth's gravity in order to enter space. Once in space it takes very little fuel and effort to move the spaceship. Now relate this to your own life and when you make a presentation. You may possibly have to give a presentation in public and you are feeling nervous. Your mind must initially overcome any negative associations you may have about giving the presentation. There may be people in the room that make you nervous. The topic of your talk may not be exciting, and it may even be bad news that you are delivering. These negative thoughts and associations are like gravity working against you and preventing your rocket from taking off the ground and then into space. How can you change these associations so that you can deliver an enthusiastic or heart felt presentation and gain the attention of the audience?

I have a dream

Think about the great orators of recent times such as the speech of Dr Martin Luther King Jr in 1963 in Washington DC in the "I have Dream speech" It was full of passion and enthusiasm that it inspired the crowd of 250,000 American people to feel the way he wanted them to feel about the civil rights movement.

Dr King was thrust worthy and people believed in him and his cause and he repeatedly said the words "I Have a Dream" toward the end of his speech to get his message across. This was important in making people really believe what he is saying. He brings a sense of unity by saying that he knows what the audience has been through because he himself has been through it.

"I am not unmindful that some of you have come here out of great trials and tribulations. Some of you have come from fresh narrow jail cells."

Dr. King's audience was inspired by him they believe that he will do everything he says. During his speech he also repeatedly uses the word **We**. This also helps to connect with the audience to say that they are in this together and shows that he is looking for the same freedom that his audience is seeking. Together they can accomplish their goals. Dr. King adds importance and emotion to his speech by having it in front of the Lincoln Memorial. It was timely since the fact that 100 years prior Lincoln signed the Emancipation Proclamation. Dr. King's enthusiastic speech is what created excitement and belief in others and his work made difference too many millions of African Americans.

Now you might be thinking "How on earth can I compare to this enthusiastic, passionate and charismatic speaker." Well the truth is that not many people can match what happened that day, yet you too have your own message for your audience. It might not be life changing and awe inspiring as Dr Kings but it's still your message to the world of your audience.

Looking back at your life can you a remember a time when you were enthusiastic about something and then as time passed by the strong feeling gradually slipped away from you. In your mind's eye visualize that the speech you are going to make. It is going to be with enthusiasm and with the intention that the information you are imparting is important to others and maybe even life changing. How much effort, courage and enthusiasm would you the muster to deliver this presentation. I am sure that you will make extra efforts to produce a great outcome. Whilst enthusiasm is a powerful emotion which helps drive us forward and involves motivation and passion you need a support system in place to ensure that it doesn't slip away.

"We deceive ourselves when we fancy that only weakness needs support. Strength needs it far more." Madame Swetchine, The Writings of Madame Swetchine

"A mediocre idea that generates enthusiasm will go further than a great idea that inspires no one." Mary Kay Ash

The challenge we may face is that too many people in our lives choose to destroy enthusiasm by sharing their own views and opinions. How many times have you been enthusiastic and passionate about something, only to find that someone else thinks differently and goes out of their way to tell you? Unless you have a strong support system in place, your enthusiasm will take a battering and before you know it your left wondering why you even felt it in the first place, "shattered dreams" It is better to tell the people that you trust and who believe in you about your ideas that way they can be supportive. The support system can take on many different forms which is personal to you. It can be a physical support in the form of a close family member or friend; it can be detached support in the form of a role model or belief system. Whatever your support system is, it needs to be in tune with the root cause of your enthusiasm for it to play a fully supporting role.

"It is not the critic who counts; not the man who points out how the strong man

stumbles, or where the doer of deeds could have done them better.

The credit belongs to the man who is actually in the arena, whose face is marred by dust and sweat and blood, who strives valiantly; who errs and comes short again and again; because there is not effort without error and shortcomings; but who does actually strive to do the deed; who knows the great enthusiasm, the great devotion, who spends himself in a worthy cause, who at the best knows in the end the triumph of high achievement and who at the worst, if he fails, at least he fails while daring greatly.

So that his place shall never be with those cold and timid souls who know neither victory nor defeat."

Theodore Roosevelt (1858 - 1919), "Man in the Arena" Speech given April 23, 1910

Enthusiasm is one of those emotions which can easily be generated but in turn by its very nature can easily be destroyed. What you do with it is entirely your choice, but whatever you do; don't underestimate the power it can have in shaping your life. Enthusiasm is one of your emotions which if displayed with true openness will influence others around you, inspiring them to act upon it.

Don't be afraid to display your enthusiasm for something. Why hold yourself back because of what others might think? Enthusiasm, passion and drive are the basis of our ever day life. However, without this drive and enthusiasm we can spiral endlessly into the day to day cycle of sameness.

"Nobody grows old merely by living a number of years. We grow old by deserting our ideals. Years may wrinkle the skin, but to give up enthusiasm wrinkles the soul." - Samuel Ullman

Tips to being more enthusiastic

1. Whatever your situation, choose to be optimistic
2. Choose to be around other enthusiastic positive minded people
3. Find something that you can be excited about
4. Be imaginative
5. Act and do

6. Never give up
7. Stay inspired by reading inspirational books
8. Stay health and energetic
9. Be grateful
10. Be Passionate

It's been a pleasure to have taken this journey with you in this Pocket book of confidence. I believe you have everything you need to achieve the confidence you seek. I said that it was written for you in mind. I sincerely wish you greater confidence so you can make your life even better and you can enhance the lives of those around you. It's you time to shine bright and let the world know who you really are. Be **courageous** and **overcome** the obstacles that face you. Stay **positive** and avoid the **negative** frogs. Summon the best **feelings** and emotions that will **inspire** you and others around you. Show the world how **determined** you are and keep boosting your **self-esteem** and do what's **necessary** to succeed. **Communicate** with abundant **enthusiasm** and passion and then you will have the confidence you need to achieve your goals.

By following the 10 GOLDEN STEPS you will change you for the better and have more courage and confidence.

1.	C	-Courage
2.	O	-Overcome
3.	N	-Negativity
4.	F	-Feelings
5.	I	-Inspiration
6.	D	-Determination
7.	E	-Esteem
8.	N	-Necessity
9.	C	-Communication
10.	E	-Enthusiasm

"Faith is the bird that feels the light when the dawn is still dark. You can't cross the sea merely by standing and staring at the water. The butterfly counts not months

but moments and has time enough."
Rabindranath Tagore

Let me know how this book has helped you and others. Take care my friend and set yourself free and go beyond your comfort zone.

confidence@pdss.co.uk

About The Author

Raj Soren was born in India in the then state of Bihar in the early 1960s. Raj and his brother moved to the UK in the 1970 to be with his parents, Dr Dhuni and Mrs. Bhagwati Soren. His father Dr Dhuni Soren is a retired GP and much respected elder statesman from Jharkhand state and an author himself in Santhal history.

Raj graduated from Manchester with a BSc honors in Biology and Chemistry and later gained a master's in business and social entrepreneurship. Raj also gained a diploma in Life coaching and has been a sales trainer as well as a manager for a top 10 pharmaceutical companies. Raj has also over 30 years coaching and examining experience for The Jiu Jitsu Foundation in the UK and has taught in countries such as Canada, USA, South Africa, Scotland, Austria, Wales, India, Fiji and in Russia as an Aikido instructor. Raj has helped thousands of individuals gain confidence through his martial arts coaching, running personal safety and anti-bullying courses and working with the Mind Charity. Raj resides in England with his wife Jyoti also a Life coach and three talented children. Suraj an Industrial Designer and working with the national mental health charity Mind, Chandni Artist and Interior designer and Lukhi Fashion Designer and founder of UnLukhi sustainable fashion brand.

Raj believes that confidence can be learnt if you are not born with it.

This Pocket book of confidence will help you gain greater confidence and overcome anchors that may be holding you back. The book encourages you to venture out of your comfort zone to try something new or something that you may shy away from doing.

The simple and effective advice contained in this book will help you become stronger in your convictions and to stay the course by understanding the reason we behave the way we do. The 10 golden steps in his book will keep you focused to achieve realistic goals.

This book will motivate and enthuse you to become a better you and help your inner voice speak up.

This book will confront excuses and anchors that may have held you back and nourish your self-esteem and build your self-belief.

The book is Interspersed with stories and anecdotes and quotes to empower you.

The best book you could buy this year as a gift to a friend or family member.

RAJ SOREN